M000310227

THE FREDERICKSB[...]

PRAYER FURNACE

THE PRIESTHOOD

THEOLOGY OF DAY AND NIGHT PRAYER

David Bradshaw

Furnace Media Group

FMG ™

WWW.THEPRAYERFURNACE.ORG

The Priesthood: Theology of Day and Night Prayer
Copyright © 2011 by Furnace Media Group
All rights reserved.

No part of this publication may be reproduced, stored in a retrieval system, or transmitted, in any form or by any means-electronic, mechanical, photocopying, recording, or otherwise copied or sold for commercial profit without prior written permission.

Version 1.1 – April 2011

Published by Furnace Media Group™
The Fredericksburg Prayer Furnace and Missions Base
P.O. Box 4117, Fredericksburg, VA 22402
furnacemedia@theprayerfurnace.org

ISBN 061-54-8721-1

Cover Design by Jimmy Maddox

Unless otherwise stated all Scripture quotations are taken from the New King James Version R. Copyright ©1982 by Thomas Nelson, Inc. Used by permission. All rights reserved.

**The Fredericksburg Prayer Furnace and
Missions Base**
www.theprayerfurnace.org

We are a missional community pursuing a vision for a perpetual solemn assembly of day and night prayer in the spirit of the Tabernacle of David, and the calling, training, and releasing of forerunner messengers and justice ministry to the lost, poor, oppressed, orphan, and widow.

Furnace Media Group
FMG™
WWW.THEPRAYERFURNACE.ORG

THE FREDERICKSBURG
PRAYER FURNACE

THE PRIESTHOOD: THEOLOGY OF DAY AND NIGHT PRAYER

TABLE OF CONTENTS

Furnace Media Group
FMG™
WWW.THEPRAYERFURNACE.ORG

Session 1: A Call to Spiritual Hunger – The Great Wisdom Clash

Therefore, behold, I will allure her, will bring her into the wilderness, and speak tenderly to her… (Hosea 2:14)

Blessed is the man whose strength is in you, whose heart is set on pilgrimage. (Psalm 84:5)

I will destroy the wisdom of the wise, and bring to nothing the understanding of the prudent. (1 Corinthians 1:19)

And the child grew and became strong in spirit, and he was in the wilderness until the days of his public appearance to Israel. (Luke 1:80)

I.   HUNGER FOR THE KNOWLEDGE OF GOD

A.   The greatest need in this hour for the church of this nation is the knowledge of God.

B.   *The low view of God entertained almost universally among Christians is the cause of a hundred lesser evils everywhere among us….with our loss of the sense of majesty has come the further loss of religious awe and consciousness of the divine Presence.*[1]

C.   Most believers live spiritually stifled lives without even knowing it. God has provided all things in Christ for a full life in the Spirit, but there is a dimension of spiritual hunger which is required to enter into this fullness. Spiritual hunger removes all the hindrances to receiving encounter with the knowledge of the holy.

D.   The pathway to fullness involves the wilderness. There are exceedingly great pleasures available to the hungry heart. The call to hunger is not about another spiritual obligation. It is a call to joy. Hunger is one of our greatest gifts in God.

---

[1] Tozer, A.W. *The Knowledge of the Holy.* San Francisco, CA: Harper pub. 1961, p. vii.

II.   THE WISDOM OF THE WILDERNESS

A. The wilderness is defined in our context as the place of intentional removal from the busyness and seductiveness of the world for the purpose of prayer and fasting. The wilderness of prayer and fasting is *intentional* weakness.

> *But he said to me, "My grace is sufficient for you, for my power is made perfect in weakness." Therefore I will boast all the more gladly about my weaknesses, so that Christ's power may rest on me. That is why, for Christ's sake, I delight in weaknesses, in insults, in hardships, in persecutions, in difficulties. For when I am weak, then I am strong. (2 Corinthians 12:9-10)*

B. God is filled with burning, jealous love. He desires to possess us completely. This is the Lord's overriding concern in dealing with us. We cannot be effective in our calling until we find satisfaction in God alone. The desperate need of the hour is men and women that have been gripped with the knowledge of God in their secret lives. We need to receive something from heaven. This only happens in the wilderness of fasting and prayer.

C. God designed the human soul to be wholehearted, abandoned, even obsessed with beauty. We will not function rightly apart from passionate pursuit of the holy.

D. Furthermore, power to shape history for the gospel does not come from within our own souls. We have no capacity to change society within ourselves. Men and women that have shaped history have all embraced a lifestyle of the wilderness, of a secret history in God, often including extended seasons of separation and prayer.

E. Developing reality in God takes time and patience. We must dial down. We must go low. God will reward the diligent seeker.

   1. Jesus spent the first thirty years of his life in hiddenness and then 40 days in the desert fasting *before* public ministry.

   2. Paul went "away into" the wilderness of Arabia before going to Jerusalem after his conversion. He delayed going to Jerusalem for 3 years, during which time he went deep in the revelation of Jesus. He speaks of being "entrusted" with the gospel. Oh, that God would raise up a generation that is entrusted with the gospel! (**Gal. 1:16-17, I Thess. 2:4**)

3. John the Baptist spent about 30 years in the wilderness praying and fasting for about 6-9 months of public ministry, followed by his martyrdom.

4. The Desert Fathers of the 4th century pioneered this lifestyle of radical consecration. A great book on this life in the Spirit is "*The Way of the Heart*" by Henri Nouwen.

F. There are two encounters in the wilderness of prayer. The wilderness is a place of encounter.

1. Yourself – usually there is a strong temptation to give up at this point. The encounter with our self and our unrenewed mind is actually an important part of our growth. Getting reality about our need for God is vital to authentic repentance and transformation. We can be real with God.

2. God – To encounter God is not to simply know more about him. It is to take on his very nature, to experience his transcendence. You begin to demonstrate that which you encounter in God. God is burning with desire and will raise up a people burning with desire for him. God is more jealous to encounter you than you are to encounter God.

Prophets are forged in the wilderness of fasting and prayer – Lou Engle

G. Our journey into the wilderness is our journey into romance and deep love for Jesus. We embrace the wilderness, not out of religious compulsion, but out of pleasure and desire. God is most glorified when we enjoy him more than any other love. As C.S. Lewis says:

"Indeed, if we consider the unblushing promises of reward and the staggering nature of the rewards promised in the Gospels, it would seem that our Lord finds our desires not too strong, but too weak. We are half-hearted creatures, fooling about with drink and sex and ambition when infinite joy is offered us, like an ignorant child who wants to go on making mud pies in a slum because he cannot imagine what is meant by the offer of a holiday at the sea. We are far too easily pleased."[2]

---

[2] Lewis, C.S. *The Weight of Glory and Other Addresses.* Grand Rapids: Eerdmans, 1965. p.1-2.

Therefore, behold, I will allure her, will bring her into the wilderness, and speak tenderly to her... (Hosea 2:14)

III. THE GREAT WISDOM CLASH

But God has chosen the foolish things of the world to put to shame the wise, and God has chosen the weak things of the world to put to shame the things which are mighty... (1 Corinthians 1:27)

A. God wars against and destroys that which man exalts. The wisdom of God is warring against what man considers to be wise.

B. The definition of wisdom is choosing the most effective and efficient means to achieve a desired goal. Most people in the Body of Christ can agree upon the goals of loving God, salvation, healing, deliverance, transformation of society, revival, etc. The clash is over how we can most effectively reach these goals.

C. In this nation, we have spent more money and energy on reaching this generation than any other nation in history and yet we are still losing a generation. Right now, 96 percent of the emerging generation in America is unchurched. There is a need for messengers that are carrying something from heaven. God has an answer: to wait on him in the wilderness of prayer and fasting.[3]

D. As Art Katz says:

"There is something about the whole structure of church life, and the necessity to perform something to justify its existence and its perpetuation, that compels it to act without waiting. There is no greater death than waiting, which is at the very heart of priestliness. Priests did not commence their priestly activity, or ministry, until seven days of waiting were completed, and the completion was the final death of their well-meaning intentions to do for God. Until that dies, there is no true priestly service, and if there is no priestly, then it is not apostolic. Jesus is the High Priest and Apostle of our confession. The first must precede the last. Impatience, self-will, religious ambition, the necessity to do and to be seen doing, to be recognized and acknowledged is death to the purpose of God.[4]"

---

[3] Rainer, Thomas. *The Bridger Generation.* Nashville, TN: Broadman & Holdman pub. 2006, p. 169

[4] Katz, Art. *Apostolic Foundations.* Laporte, MN: Burning Bush pub. 1999. p. 11.

4

E.   God's strength is made perfect in only one place: man's weakness. It is in our leaning into God with awareness of desperate need that we encounter him and experience his strength. By this we glorify God, as we lean on him, as we look to him. Jesus called this being "poor in spirit."

...my strength is made perfect in weakness. (1 Corinthians 12:9)

Blessed are the poor in spirit for theirs is the kingdom of heaven. (Matthew 5:3)

F.   This is the wisdom of focused lifestyles of fasting, prayer, and spiritual hunger. We are able to receive grace in the context of our weakness. The lifestyle that Jesus teaches in the Sermon on the Mount (Matt. 5-7) is precisely this and requires an eternal perspective. God acts on behalf of those who wait for him.

G.   Ultimately, the wisdom of God is the cross and total abandonment. God's wisdom is to lose your life completely and to be found in Christ. The secret of Christianity is when Christ fully possesses men. God did not call you to be "strong" according the worldly definition. He has called you to pursue strength according to heaven's definition.

IV.   JOHN THE BAPTIST – FORERUNNER OF THE WILDERNESS

And the child [John the Baptist] grew and became strong in spirit, and was in the deserts till the day of his manifestation to Israel. (Luke 1:80)

Assuredly, I say to you, among those born of a woman there has not risen one greater than John the Baptist...For since the time of John the Baptist until now the kingdom of heaven suffers violence and the violent take it by force. (Matthew 11:11-12)

A.   John the Baptist lived in the desert. This lifestyle was simply for the purpose of prayer. He came neither eating nor drinking, meaning he fasted regularly (Matt 11:18). His lifestyle was a prophetic word to Israel. John was not motivated by guilt and fear but burning desire and prophetic vision. John was in touch with a higher pleasure and a deeper reality.

B.   John the Baptist had a "day of manifestation" to Israel (**Luke 1:80**). John didn't simply have a message. He was the message. Because of his extravagant love, Jesus called him the greatest man ever born of a woman!

Assuredly, I say to you, among those born of a woman there has not risen one greater than John the Baptist… (Matthew 11:11)

C.   John's life is extremely relevant to us in this generation. Even as his life was a sign and wonder to Israel to prepare for Jesus' first coming, there is going to be another even greater manifestation of the "spirit of Elijah," which John walked in, through the church in the generation of the Lord's return.

Behold, I will send you Elijah the prophet <u>before the great and terrible day of the Lord</u> comes. (Malachi 4:5)

…and he [John] will go before him in the spirit and power of Elijah. (Luke 1:17)

D.   The "spirit of Elijah" is six-fold in its manifestation. These six realities are being released even in this season on the church globally:

1.   **Radical lifestyles** of prayer and fasting – Elijah was known for prayer. **(James 5:17-18)**

2.   **Bold preaching** that confronts the antichrist system with the love of Jesus.

3.   **Signs and wonders** on scale the surpasses both the book of Acts and Exodus.

4.   **Generational healing** through a revelation of Abba, Father.

5.   An **emphasis on the first commandment** being in first place (confronting idolatry – Example: Elijah and the prophets of Baal on Mount Carmel).

6.   **Consecration and holiness** (superior pleasures in God).

E.   John was not under a religious spirit. He was not striving in bondage. He was constrained by love. His spirit of revelation actually made war on the religious spirit of man-pleasing and fear that consumed the spiritual leadership of his day. He lived radically before the Lord with his primary motive being desire for the Bridegroom. His lifestyle, intercessions, and message served to prepare the way for Jesus' coming. The Lord will not come again without a clear prophetic voice on the earth.

> ***Your people shall be volunteers in the day of Your power. (Psalm 110:3)***

F. The enemy would seek, at times, to associate radical lifestyle with legalism or error (even as they did with John the Baptist). But, in fact, this lifestyle is rooted in love and motivated by a spirit of revelation, which overcomes the religious spirit. Love will take the human spirit to higher heights than fear.

> ***[18] For John came neither eating nor drinking, and they say, 'He has a demon.' (Matthew (11:18)***

V.   SPIRITUAL VIOLENCE

> ***[12] And from the days of John the Baptist until now the kingdom of heaven suffers violence, and the violent take it by force. (Matthew 11:12)***

A. The principle of <u>spiritual violence</u>: There are certain dimensions in the grace of God that are only available to the hungry and require radical lifestyles.

B. Christ has purchased every spiritual blessing for us, but because of the falleness of our hearts, our unrenewed minds, and the distractions of the world and the enemy, it takes "violence" to enter into fullness. John's lifestyle of fasting was an expression of spiritual hunger and was a testimony to "more than meets the eye."

> ***John answered and said, "A man can receive nothing unless it has been given to him from heaven." (John 3:27)***

C. Violent *pursuit* of the fullness of God is the only logical response to the magnitude of what God has made available to us.

D. Jesus called this the "narrow way." It is difficult, but filled with the pleasures of God. The ability to walk in spiritual violence is still by grace and not by the flesh. Our flesh cannot accomplish righteousness. It is the grace of God through the power of the Spirit that we enter into the fullness of God. Spiritual violence is not about earning but more deeply receiving.

> ***Enter by the narrow gate. For the gate is wide and the way is easy that leads to destruction, and those who enter by it are many. For the gate is narrow and the way is hard that leads to life, and those who find it are few. (Matthew 7:13-14)***

E.   Desire is the currency of heaven.

> *The hunger of a man's soul must be satisfied. It must be satisfied. It is the law of God; that law of God is in the depth of the Spirit. God will answer the heart that cries. God will answer that soul that asks. Christ Jesus comes to us with divine assurance and invites us when we are hungry to pray, to believe, to take from the Lord that which our soul covets and our heart asks for. (John G. Lake)*[5]

> **Blessed are those who hunger and thirst for righteousness, for they shall be filled. (Matthew 5:6)**

> **You open Your hand and satisfy the desire of every living thing. (Psalm 145:16)**

F.   A hidden life like John experienced is preparation for manifestation. We are made relevant by our secret history with God.

> **For you died and your life is hidden with Christ in God. (Colossians 3:3)**

G.   Contrary to popular opinion, John the Baptist was an extremely joyful man. He was the first person in history to refer to Jesus as a Bridegroom. His motivation was joy. His reality was deep love. The wilderness was his place of communion with the Beloved.

> **He who has the bride is the bridegroom; but the friend of the bridegroom, who stands and hears him, rejoices greatly because of the bridegroom's voice. <u>Therefore this joy of mine is fulfilled.</u> He must increase, but I must decrease. (John 3:29-30)**

VI.   JESUS' DESIRE

> **Father, I desire that they also whom You gave Me may be with Me where I am, that they may behold My glory which You have given Me; for You loved Me before the foundation of the world. O righteous Father! The world has not**

---

[5] Lake, John G. *John G. Lake: The Complete Collection of His Life Teachings.* ed. Roberts Liardon. New Kensington: Whitaker House Pub., 1999. p. 455

known You, but I have known You; and these have known that You sent Me. And I have declared to them Your name, and will declare it, <u>that the love with which You loved Me may be in them, and I in them</u>. (John 17:24-26)

A.   Jesus is filled with desire. His desire is that we would be with him, see his glory, and love him with all our hearts. Until our life is oriented around this great pursuit, we will never fulfill our true destiny. Many go into the wilderness of fasting and prayer because they want success in ministry or business, but these are the secondary rewards. The first goal on God's mind is this: that we would love Jesus like the Father loves Jesus.

B.   You are not here because you desire God, but because he first desired you. He wants to meet you and show himself to you more than you do. Do you know this God, the God of desire for you? Do you know the God who fully intends to sweep you off your feet? Our *only* means by which we can grow in radical consecration and lifestyles of passionate pursuit is by first experiencing the Father's deep love. Our love is simply a response. We already made it, so now we can reach for the fullness that Jesus dies to gives us!

I am my beloved's, and his desire is toward me. (Song of Solomon 7:10)

Therefore, behold, <u>I will allure her</u>, will bring her into the wilderness, and speak tenderly to her… (Hosea 2:14)

His eyes were like a flame of fire… (Rev. 19:12)

That was the true Light [Jesus] which gives light to every man coming into the world. (John 1:9)

The better a man learns to pray, the more deeply he finds that all his stammering is only an answer to God's speaking to him…For we have been permitted to glimpse his inner nature, to enter into it, into the inner core of eternal truth; bathed in this light which radiates upon us from God, we ourselves become light and transparent before him. (Hans Urs Von Balthasar)[6]

---

[6] Von Balthasar, Hans Urs. *Prayer.* San Francisco: Ignatius Press, 1986. p. 14-15.

C.   This is good news. Your encounter with God is guaranteed because Jesus prayed for it and ultimately laid down his life for you to encounter and experience the depths of God. The veil to the Holy of Holies was torn when Jesus died. He was literally crucified to purchase communion with you forever. What love! We can come with total confidence, extreme boldness, and faith.

D.   There is often a season of obedience before you experience deep encounter with God. But Jesus promises to manifest (reveal, show) himself to you.

He who has My commandments and keeps them, it is he who loves Me. And he who loves Me will be loved by My Father, and I will love him and manifest Myself to him. (John 14:21)

E.   Do not despise the small movements of the heart. Those small movements of desire for God and love are supernatural and transform your heart. All you have to do is position yourself to gaze on (give undivided attention to) God. You will be transfigured into his very image. You were made to carry glory, to shine glory, as an image bearer of God.

But we all, with unveiled face, beholding as in a mirror the glory of the Lord, are being transformed into the same image from glory to glory, just as by the Spirit of the Lord. (2 Cor. 3:18)

VI.   TOOLS FOR THE JOURNEY (5 KEYS)

A.   Meditation on the Word

1.   The greatest key to the spirit of revelation is long and loving meditation on the Word.

2.   God is changing the way we relate to the Word of God. For many of us, the Bible is a set of doctrines that we are "required" to learn in order to grow. This book is more than philosophy. It is the open door to encounter the person of Christ himself. The Bible is not boring, you're boring!

3.   RWSSP! (Read it, Write it, Sing it, Say it, Pray it)

They said to each other, 'Did not our hearts burn within us while he talked to us on the road, while he opened to us the Scriptures?' (Luke 24:8)

B.   Praying in the Spirit

He who speaks in a tongue edifies himself... (1 Corinthians 14:4)

I thank God that I speak with tongues more than you all. (1 Corinthians 14:18)

1.   I encourage people to pray in the Spirit (tongues) for at least two hours per day. This will unlock a wellspring of revelation and the knowledge of God. As you fellowship with the Holy Spirit in this way, you begin to receive his nature in your soul.

2.   The benefits of praying and singing in tongues are manifold. It releases the life of God in the inner man (1 Cor. 14:4). It releases power for ministry and spiritual warfare (Eph. 6:18).

3.   In spite of all the attention this gift gets, it is possibly the most underused gift because many assume that since they "have it" they don't need to really use it.

4.   Paul had a high value for tongues. He valued this gift so much that he sought to provoke the Corinthian church to prayer by proclaiming that he prayed in tongues more than anyone else that he knew!

C.   Silence

1.   Silence is the home of the Word. Times of silence or "soaking" is critical to intimacy with God.

2.   Silence is often the context of some of the deepest encounters with God.

3.   St. Teresa of Avila, one of the greatest voices on deep prayer, said that the best way to engage in communion with God is to *focus your mind on the "indwelling presence" and simply not say anything.*

4.   Other options: Focus on the Throne Room (Rev. 4-5), picture a biblical story, let the Holy Spirit give you visions.

D. Dialog

1. The biblical model for prayer is "without ceasing." Talk to the Lord all the time!

   Pray without ceasing. (1 Thessalonians 5:17)

2. Brother Lawrence called this concept of unbroken dialog "practicing the presence of God" which means to maintain a constant awareness of God's presence in you and with you at all times.

3. Henri Nouwen speaks of turning your thoughts into conversation with the Divine Spirit.

4. I also encourage people to have a basic list that they pray from.

5. MAKE A PLAN for your prayer room time!

E. Fasting

1. Nothing tenderizes the heart and opens a person to encounter with God like adding fasting to your prayer life.

2. Fasting is a vital part of revelation and encounter. Many saints have fasted on a weekly basis for their entire Christian experience.

Session 2: Introduction to the Priesthood: Understanding Our Identity and Function

To him who loves us and has freed us from our sins by his blood and <u>made us a kingdom, priests to his God and Father</u>, to him be glory and dominion forever and ever. Amen. (Revelation 1:5-6)

'You will be for me <u>a kingdom of priests</u> and a holy nation.' These are the words you are to speak to the Israelites. (Exodus 19:6)

Coming to Him as to a living stone, rejected indeed by men, but chosen by God and precious, you also, as living stones, are being built up a spiritual house, <u>a holy priesthood, to offer up spiritual sacrifices acceptable to God through Jesus Christ</u>. (1 Peter 2:4)

I. OVERVIEW

    A.   Priestly ministry is our eternal calling and our greatest privilege. God has always intended for every believer to have access to himself through one mediator, his Son, Jesus Christ. At the very foundation of the gospel is the revelation of the priesthood of every believer. Martyrs of old went to their executions over this doctrine. Yet very few consider the implications of this doctrine, and fewer still actually experience any kind of fullness in their priestly calling.

    B.   Much of the church is suffering an identity crisis. We do not know who we are before the Lord. We frequently find our identity in secondary things. Our core identity and first ministry is as priests before God. This was so important to God that Jesus' blood was shed to purchase this ministry for us.

    C.   God has always desired that *all* his people be priests not just one portion or tribe. This is our glorious privilege in Jesus. The veil was torn when Jesus died. God's desire was for human beings to dwell with him and share his heart in an unprecedented level of intimacy and authority.

        To him who loves us and has freed us from our sins by his blood and <u>made us a kingdom, priests to his God and Father</u>. (Revelation 1:5-6)

D. Understanding our priestly calling shifts us from an external focus to valuing things that are unseen more than what we can see in the natural. Our true life is hidden with Christ. Our primary focus is to be on things that are, for the most part, unseen in this age.

E. To walk in our priestly calling is to experience our heavenly calling, to engage the throne room and the One seated on the throne.

Set your mind on things above, not on things on the earth. (Colossians 3:2)

Therefore, holy brethren, partakers of a heavenly calling…(Hebrews 3:1)

Let us therefore come boldly to the throne of grace, that we may obtain mercy and find grace to help in time of need. (Hebrews 4:16)

F. Priestly ministry shifts us from an event orientation to a lifestyle of communion with God and encounter. Priestly ministry is a lifestyle. Daniel prayed three times per day "since his youth." David ministered to the Lord seven times per day. The priests of old had a rhythm of life before the Lord, which created a context for God and man to fellowship on an ongoing intimate basis and for the Lord to manifest his power.

G. The Old Covenant Levitical priesthood was but a type and shadow of the greater priestly ministry we have in Christ. We often think the other way around - that our priestly ministry is a shadow of the Old Covenant priests. Reality is, however, that our priestly ministry in Christ is the reality of which they were prophesying.

For Christ has not entered the holy places made with hands, which are copies of the true things… (Hebrews 9:24)

For the law, having a shadow of the good things to come, and not the very image of the things, can never with these same sacrifices, which they offer continually year by year, make those who approach perfect. (Hebrews 10:1)

H. True spiritual authority comes from priestly ministry. Priestly ministry is always our first ministry, and all true apostolic ministry flows from the priestly. Jesus is our Great High Priest and Apostle – perfectly combining the priestly and the kingly (apostolic). We are being conformed to his very image on the earth. He is the first born among many brothers. We share his ministry in the priesthood.

...and he will be a priest on his throne... (Zechariah 6:13)

...the LORD has sworn and will not relent, "You [Jesus] are a priest forever, according to the order of Melchizedek..." (Psalm 110:5-6)

Therefore, holy brethren, partakers of a heavenly calling, consider Jesus, the Apostle and High Priest of our calling. (Hebrews 3:1)

I.   "Until God shall inspire and restore in us a true sense of priestliness, we will not be partaking in a calling that is heavenly. The word 'heavenly' does not refer to something spatial, but to a mindset, a mentality, or a mode of being...there is a requirement to minister unto God *before* one ministers to men. If we lack the sense of the sacredness of God, which is to be found only in the holy place, by those who have the posture of a priest, that is to say, prostrated as a dead man before him, then there is going to be something brittle, something lacking, something plastic in the ministry we bring. There is a cry of God for the restoration of the priesthood that alone will save us from the superficial demonstrations that ostensibly performed in his name."[7]

J.   Kings are remembered for their accomplishments, but priests are remembered for their lifestyles. Kings are known on the earth and priests are known in heaven. Because the primary interaction of a priest's life is directly with the Lord, the way he/she will be known is not primarily what the 'newspapers' say about him or her but what God and the angels will say. This was the calling on the priests of old and most of their testimonies are hidden in their intimacy with God and not with us or in our history books. (Kirk Bennett)

K.   There are four specific dimensions to our priestly ministry as believers in Jesus:

  1.   **Intimacy** - access to the manifest glory of God to stand, behold, and encounter

    One thing I ask of the Lord, this is what I seek; that I may dwell in the house of the Lord all the days of my life, to gaze on the beauty of the Lord and to seek him in his temple. (Psalm 27:4)

    But he who is joined to the Lord is one spirit with Him. (1 Corinthians 6:17)

---

[7] Katz, Art. *Apostolic Foundations.* Laporte, MN: Burning Bush Pub, 1999. pp. 22-23.

He who has the bride is the bridegroom; but the friend of the   bridegroom, who stands and hears him, rejoices greatly because of the bridegroom's voice. Therefore this joy of mine is fulfilled. (John 3:29)

2.   **Worship/Ministry to the Lord** – Extravagant Love

But you are a chosen generation, <u>a royal priesthood</u>, a holy nation, His own special people, <u>that you may proclaim the praises</u> of Him who called you out of darkness into His marvelous light. (1 Peter 2:9)

But the priests, the Levites, the sons of Zadok, who kept charge of My sanctuary when the children of Israel went astray from Me, they shall come near Me to minister to Me; and they shall stand before Me…(Ezekiel 44:15)

    a)   Music takes a significant role in our priestly ministry even as it did in the priestly ministry of the Old Covenant.

3.   **Intercession** – Government and Mediation

    a)   Prayer is not just the side activity that we do to help our real work in ministry. It is real work and real ministry. We must understand that fruitfulness flows from the place of prayer. Our ministry is simply a manifestation of answered prayer.

Ask of Me and I will make the nations your inheritance…(Psalm 2:8)

Gather the people, Sanctify the congregation, Assemble the elders, gather the children and nursing babes; Let the bridegroom go out from his chamber, And the bride from her dressing room. <u>Let the priests, who minister to the LORD, Weep between the porch and the altar; Let</u> them say, "Spare Your people, O LORD, And do not give Your heritage to reproach, That the nations should rule over them. Why should they say among the peoples, "Where is their God?" (Joel 2:16-17)

4.   **Prophecy** - Forerunner Messengers (anointing of the Spirit)

For the lips of a priest should keep knowledge, And people should seek the law from his mouth; For <u>he is the messenger of the LORD</u> of hosts. (Malachi 2:7)

> *The words of Jeremiah, the son of Hilkiah, one of the priests...to whom the word of the Lord came... (Jeremiah 1:1-2)*

L.   God will cover the entire earth with this kind of priestly ministry before Jesus comes back. This is the context of global revival and end-time judgments.

> *"My name will be great among the nations, from the rising to the setting of the sun. In every place incense and pure offerings will be brought to my name, because my name will be great among the nations," says the LORD Almighty. (Malachi 1:11)*

II. CREATED FOR INTIMACY AND DOMINION (GENESIS 1:1-28)

A.   Each according to its kind

1.   The uncreated God, who has existed from all eternity, is completely self-sufficient within himself. However, out of the overflow of his love and joy within himself, God created the heavens and the earth. He created all living things according to a pattern - an original and a counterpart. Out of the union of two, new life would be birthed and fruitfulness would come.

2.   When God came to this pinnacle of his creation, he created image bearers, human beings. He is the original. We are the counterpart. Out of our union and intimacy with him, life would flow.

> *Then God said, "Let Us make man in Our image, according to Our likeness; let them have dominion over the fish of the sea, over the birds of the air, and over the cattle, over all the earth and over every creeping thing that creeps on the earth." So God created man in His own image; in the image of God He created him; male and female He created them. Then God blessed them, and God said to them, "Be fruitful and multiply; fill the earth and subdue it; have dominion over the fish of the sea, over the birds of the air, and over every living thing that moves on the earth." (Genesis 1:26-28)*

3.   God did this out of the overflow of His desire for partnership and intimacy. You were made for God. We were created for deep fellowship with God and to rule over the created order in love. This is an unthinkable reality. Man was created to

have dominion over all the created order in union with the Triune God. No other created being comes close to this privilege.

4. Even human marriage speaks of a greater union: Christ and the church (**Ephesians 5:32**). We are the only created being which will experience this complete union with God. Beloved, we do not know who we are!

B.   God breathed into his nostrils

    1.   In Genesis 2:7, God Himself formed man out of clay and breathed into his nostrils; the clay became a living being. Adam lived and breathed out of this intimacy, this is what gave him dominion over all of created order.

    2.   The Bible begins with God creating Adam and giving him dominion over all the creation. God brought all the animals to him to name and govern. Adam functioned in partnership with God. Adam only lost this dominion when he bought into the satanic lie that he could function independently of God.

    3.   At the end, the praying church will release the great judgments of God on the antichrist, global revival, and the second coming of Jesus. God has sovereignly determined to exercise his government in partnership with humans forever.

    4.   The central theme of the scriptures is God searching for a man and a people with whom he can fully share his heart and emotions – so that they can identify with him and represent him. This revealing of his secrets is more than just giving information to people about God's plans, it is a sharing of his burden, his emotions, his thoughts, his will, on the deepest level. There is no other created being (including all the angelic orders) that can come close to this intimacy.

    For the Lord GOD does nothing without revealing his secret to his servants the prophets. (Amos 3:7)

    Justice is turned back, and righteousness stands far away; for truth has stumbled in the public squares, and uprightness cannot enter. Truth is lacking, and he who departs from evil makes himself a prey. The LORD saw it, and it displeased him that there was no justice. He saw that there was no man, and wondered that there was no one to intercede; then his own arm brought him salvation, and his righteousness upheld him. (Isaiah 59:14-16)

5. The Lord is searching to close the gap between heaven and earth, between his heart and ours. There is a longing in him to restore and surpass what he created in the garden of Eden.

6. Our premise: God has always been searching for an intercessor. He has sovereignly chosen to manifest his kingdom through human partnership.

C. In the fullness of time, God sent his Son as the Intercessor.

1. Jesus is fully God and fully man. He could sympathize completely with man's plight and God's burning desire. God found his intercessor to close the gap and bring Heaven and Earth together.

2. Jesus' death, resurrection, and ascension was and is the greatest act of intercession that has ever been seen. Angels stand in wonder, elders worship, kings will shut their mouth and the redeemed weep with gratitude at this one who placed his body in the gap between the wrath of God and a lost humanity to give us access to the Father. Jesus identified fully with man in our weakness and was filled with sympathy for us, and he also identified fully with God's justice. Therefore, he acted as our perfect high priest.

3. Because of Jesus' priestly ministry, we now have perfect access and fellowship with the Father. Jesus opened the way through his blood for our priestly ministry and we can come with boldness and confidence before the very throne of God in intimacy and intercession.

Therefore, brothers, since we have confidence to enter the holy places by the blood of Jesus, by a new and living way that he opened for us through the curtain, that is, through his flesh, and since we have a great high priest over the house of God, let us draw near with a true heart in full assurance of faith, with our hearts sprinkled clean from an evil conscience and our bodies washed with pure water. (Hebrews 10:19-22)

4. Even now, Jesus ever lives to intercede. He is a priest forever. We are being conformed to his image, and we will enter to his very intercession at

the throne of God. We are caught up in the whirlwind of God's emotions and join Jesus in his ministry of intercession.

> ***Therefore He is also able to save to the uttermost those who come to God through Him, since He always lives to make intercession for them. (Hebrews 7:25)***

D.   Summary: The Lord has always sought intercessors. An intercessor is caught up in the whirlwind of God's emotions. God is filled with righteousness and is, therefore, angry at all sin. He is filled with hatred for sin because of its destruction of all that is good. He has to judge sin, and therefore, sinners. He is also filled with compassion and love for his creation, and especially the image bearers. To join Jesus in intercession is to live in this place of intimacy with him and to stand in the gap between God's holiness and man's fallenness. This is our calling.

III.   PRIESTLY IDENTITY: INTIMACY AND SONSHIP

A.   Our identity as priests is rooted in the affections of the Father and the Bridegroom for us. The One seated on the throne is our "Abba, Father." He is filled with tender love, which surpasses that which fallen father's have for their children. In Christ, we have already arrived. We are sons forever. Our priestly ministry is his life and his priestly ministry being expressed through us.

B.   Identity is that which we look to for value as a person. What gives us fulfillment? How do we define success? Do we embrace God's definition of success? As Mike Bickle says, "We are loved and we are lovers, therefore we are successful."

C.   God defines greatness by the movements of the heart in love. This is at the core of priestly ministry.

> ***For the LORD does not see as man sees; for man looks at the outward appearance, but the LORD looks at the heart. (1 Samuel 16:7)***

D.   Priesthood comes from lineage. It was the sons of Aaron, the sons of Zadok, the sons of Levi. Our identity as beloved sons is the foundation of our priestly calling. God specifically states that Jesus' high priestly role flowed from his position before the Father as the Beloved Son. There is no priestly ministry apart from sonship. We have been "begotten of God" through the new birth. We are not trying to gain acceptance from the Father in our priestly ministry, but we are simply moving in a place of total acceptance and authority through the finished work of Christ.

So Christ did not exalt himself to be made a high priest, but was appointed by him who said to him, "You are my Son, today I have begotten you"; as he says in another place, "You are a priest forever after the order of Melchizedek." (Hebrews 5:5-6)

E.   As priests, we call on the Name of the Lord. It is the name (or nature) of God himself that forms the foundation of our priestly calling and ministry. Our priestly ministry flows from the revelation of the name of the Lord, or his attributes, his nature, his personality. The key our life in the Spirit is experiencing God's *personality*.

F.   Jesus' highest ministry was to reveal the Name of the Father to us. This will result in the love of the Trinity being placed with us! So, this is the very foundation of priestly ministry. God will reveal God to your spirit to awe and stun you forever with his excellent splendor.

Father, I desire that they also whom You gave Me may be with Me where I am, that they may behold My glory which You have given Me; for You loved Me before the foundation of the world. O righteous Father! The world has not known You, but I have known You; and these have known that You sent Me. And I have declared to them Your name, and will declare it, that the love with which You loved Me may be in them, and I in them. (John 17:24-26)

And the LORD passed before him and proclaimed, "The LORD, the LORD God, merciful and gracious, longsuffering, and abounding in goodness and truth, keeping mercy for thousands, forgiving iniquity and transgression and sin, by no means clearing the guilty, visiting the iniquity of the fathers upon the children and the children's children to the third and the fourth generation." (Exodus 34:6-7)

1.   **The LORD** – "Yahweh" – God is the sovereign king. He is ruler of the kings of the earth. He is omniscient and omnipotent.

To give a very brief glimpse into the omnipotence of God:

It would take the Gross National Product (GNP) of the U.S. 7 million years for one power company to run the sun for 1 second .

There are billions upon billions of stars in the universe. The largest star that we know of could fit about 7 quadrillion earths in the one star. To give a sense of how large that is:

A million seconds ago = 12 days ago
A billion seconds ago = 32 years ago
A trillion seconds ago = 31,709 years ago
A quadrillion seconds ago = 30,800,000 years ago

And the Lord did this all with one word.

2. **Merciful** – The Lord delights in mercy. He stoops to care for the weak and the undeserving. Jesus gave up his rights and his equality with the Father to express mercy to his enemies and save whosoever will come to him.

3. **Gracious** – The Father gives good gifts. He is extravagant beyond our wildest imaginations. He is kind in *all* his deeds (**Ps. 145:17**)

4. **Longsuffering** – God is slow to anger. He even gives Jezebel time to repent (**Rev. 2:21**).

5. **Abounding in goodness** – Goodness is God's very nature. He overflows with all that is good and pleasing. All that we receive is from an overflowing One that is all-powerful and totally good and kind.

6. **Keeping mercy for thousands** – God has stored up mercy for the nations, for all that will call upon him. He waits to show mercy. He literally dreams up ways to show mercy – the cross being the highest and most extravagant act of mercy that could possibly be conceived.

7. **Forgiving iniquity** – Jesus' blood has removed our guilt before the Father and has given us a new righteous nature.

8. **By no means clearing the guilty** – He will punish openly all that will not repent. In his zeal for love and truth, he must destroy those that hinder love.

9. **Visiting iniquity of fathers on children** – He is a righteous judge that will even punish children for sins of their parents in order to keep the sin

from perpetuating and destroying more lives. This is actually God's mercy in preserving righteousness.

IV.   ZEAL FOR HIS HOUSE: GOD'S DESIRE FOR A PRIESTHOOD

Father, I desire that they also whom You gave Me may be with Me where I am, that they may behold My glory which You have given Me; for You loved Me before the foundation of the world. O righteous Father! The world has not known You, but I have known You; and these have known that You sent Me. And I have declared to them Your name, and will declare it, <u>that the love with which You loved Me may be in them, and I in them</u>. (John 17:24-26)

A.   Jesus' High Priestly prayer demonstrates the passion of God at the very core of the gospel. He is filled with zeal for his house, which is the church. He is filled with burning desire for nearness with humans. The priestly ministry is the answer to Jesus' desire for nearness.

B.   Jesus is consumed (or 'eaten up') with zeal for union with the Bride. It is in the impartation of this zeal that we find our priestly ministry and our identity. There is no way to live radically without a revelation of Jesus' burning desire and affection. Human, fleshly zeal will only and ultimately lead to burnout.

   Then His disciples remembered that it was written, "Zeal for Your house has eaten Me up." (John 2:17)

   Father I desire…. (John 17:24)

C.   The house of prayer was Jesus' idea as the Great High Priest of our faith. <u>The house of prayer is his action plan to fulfill his unyielding passion.</u>

   I am my beloved's, and his desire is toward me. (Song of Solomon 7:10)

V.   PRIESTLY CHARACTER: MEEKNESS

Let this mind be in you which was also in Christ Jesus, who, being in the form of God, did not consider it robbery to be equal with God, but made Himself of no reputation, taking the form of a bondservant, and coming in the likeness of men. And being found in appearance as a man, He humbled Himself and became obedient to the point of death, even the death of the cross. Therefore God also has highly exalted

Him and given Him the name which is above every name, that at the name of Jesus every knee should bow, of those in heaven, and of those on earth, and of those under the earth, and that every tongue should confess that Jesus Christ is Lord, to the glory of God the Father. (Philippians 2:5-11)

A. Priesthood is meekness. It is to lay down your life for others' good without looking to personal comfort and happiness. Meekness is defined as using our resources for the good of others not our personal gain. Paradoxically, this works towards our good in the end. The Lord clearly states that he exalts the humble.

   But He gives more grace. Therefore He says: "God resists the proud, but gives grace to the humble." (James 4:6)

   Humble yourselves in the sight of the Lord, and He will lift you up. (James 4:10)

   But he who is greatest among you shall be your servant. And whoever exalts himself will be humbled, and he who humbles himself will be exalted. (Matthew 23:11-12)

B. Meekness is greatness. Meekness is the center of priestly character. I encourage people to pursue meekness and intimacy with Jesus as the *primary* focus of their personal life. This is the highest grace in life.

C. Humility, meekness, and servanthood are all sides of the same coin. Humility before God is the heart of intimacy with him. Prayer is the ultimate expression of humility because it expresses our total dependence on him.

Session 3: David's Vow – The Tabernacle of David and the Resting Place

Give ear and come to me, hear me, that your soul may live. I will make an everlasting covenant with you, my faithful love promised to David. See, I have made him a <u>witness to the peoples</u>, a leader and commander of the peoples. (Isaiah 55:3-4)

Remember, O LORD, in David's favor, all the hardships he endured, how he swore to the LORD and vowed to the Mighty One of Jacob, "I will not enter my house or get into my bed, I will not give sleep to my eyes or slumber to my eyelids, <u>until I find a place for the LORD a dwelling place for the Mighty One of Jacob</u>"…Arise, O LORD, and go to your resting place, you and the ark of your might. Let your priests be clothed with righteousness, and let your saints shout for joy. For the sake of your servant David, do not turn away the face of your anointed one. (Psalm 132:1-10)

I.   DAVID'S VOW

A. David's throne is the throne that Jesus will sit upon. Christ is the "son of David." Therefore, it was imperative that David exemplify the core values and passion of the kingdom of the Messiah. David's leadership was a watershed moment in redemptive history as the messianic monarchy was established by God through his leadership.

B. Isaiah 55 speaks of David as a "witness" to the peoples. He was a sign and wonder in the earth. He was a demonstration of the value system of the kingdom of God on two levels.

1. David was an example or witness of how God deals with weak people that are truly repentant. He was a revelation of the tenderness, kindness, and mercy of God.

2. David was an example of what the Lord is searching for in the hearts of men. He was the man after God's own heart. In this sense, he is a model for us even today.

   The LORD has sought for Himself a man [David] after His own heart, and the LORD has commanded him to be commander over His people, because you have not kept what the LORD commanded you." (1 Samuel 13:14)

C. Central to David's value system was his passion for God's <u>manifest glory</u> to dwell with Israel in Jerusalem. He was consumed with this vision that was God's original purpose in the creation of man – to find a dwelling place with the image bearers. This was David's first priority as king.

I will not enter my house or get into my bed, I will not give sleep to my eyes or slumber to my eyelids, <u>until I find a place for the LORD a dwelling place for the Mighty One of Jacob.</u> (Psalm 132:3-5)

For zeal for your house has consumed me…(Psalm 69:9)

D. David made an actual vow to not live "business as usual" until God had a dwelling place on earth. David knew that God burned with passion to manifest himself in and through his people. He would not pursue his own comfort when the Lord was not resting in glory among the people of Israel. God is raising up a prophetic church that will walk out David's vow in their personal lives and the corporate expression of the church. This involves a radical re-orientation of our lifestyles, how we use time and money, and how we live together.

E. David is a picture of what God is releasing on the church at the end of the age. History began with a resting place of God with men (Gen. 1-2) and it will end with a full manifestation of God's dwelling with men (Rev. 20-22).

II.   GOD'S RESTING PLACE: A DEFINITION

A. God's resting place is the manifestation of the glory (Kabod) of God with and in human beings. It is the glory of Christ being experienced and expressed by humans. When the glory of God is dwelling with a people, shadows heal people, there is unity, and the knowledge of God is poured out. When we speak of the glory of God resting, we are speaking of a weighty, tangible presence of God through the Holy Spirit.

"And it shall come to pass in the last days," says God, "that I will pour out of My Spirit on all flesh" (Acts 2:17)

B. When God is "resting" with a corporate people, his power is manifest openly which involves the gifts of the Spirit being present in fullness.

C. God's resting place is a context where we are no longer striving against him but are living in 100 percent obedience and agreement with his heart. This is where he is at rest among a people, and therefore, tangibly present among them. Currently, God is striving with most of his people most of the time (Is. 63:10).

But they rebelled and grieved His Holy Spirit; so He turned Himself against them as an enemy, and He fought against them. (Isaiah 63:10)

D. David was a "wise master builder" even as was the Apostle Paul. He understood that there is a specific context in which God will dwell in manifest glory. Paul was building something very specific in his apostolic ministry: a resting place for God. There are biblical pre-conditions for a resting place for God.

According to the grace of God which was given to me, as a wise master builder I have laid the foundation, and another builds on it. But let each one take heed how he builds on it. (1 Corinthains 3:10)

...in whom you also are being built together for a dwelling place of God in the Spirit. (Ephesians 2:22)

E. Revival does not and will not happen in a vacuum. David built with his highest priority being creating a context where God could move in power and where the knowledge of God was central. This is the apostolic pattern.

F. God's resting place is **_corporate_** and **_geographic_** (transformation). Biblically, we are the resting place for God. We are the temple. So we cannot receive any more of the Holy Spirit than we already have in our spirit. But there is also a biblical/historical reality of peoples and regions where God is *manifestly* resting. These are usually referred to as revival centers, but there is a specific context where God is being experienced openly in the mind, will, and emotions of a people and in glory and power in a region.

G. God will not change who he is for Americans. I believe that there is not currently a resting place for the manifest glory of God in America.

H. Great Dilemma: If God dwells in power, he will destroy all that resists him. When God comes in power, he is who he is, and he is a consuming fire. It is his mercy at times that he withholds his fullness!

...for our God is a consuming fire. (Hebrews 12:29)

III. SUPERNATURAL GENERATIONS: BIBLICAL EXAMPLES OF THE RESTING PLACE

A. In the Old Testament, there was only one true resting place: the Holy of Holies. Only the high priest could enter this once per year. It was God's mercy that he placed so much protocol around his presence. The Holy of Holies was a gloriously dangerous place.

B. The generation of Moses experienced a resting place of the glory of God. Every person in the community of Israel experienced the manifest glory of God and the breakthrough of power on a regular basis. When the Lord is resting with a people, the stakes go up in terms of the standard of obedience as we see in the life of Moses.

"And I will send My Angel before you, and I will drive out the Canaanite and the Amorite and the Hittite and the Perizzite and the Hivite and the Jebusite. Go up to a land flowing with milk and honey; for I will not go up in your midst, lest I consume you on the way, for you are a stiff-necked people." And when the people heard this bad news, they mourned... And it came to pass, when Moses entered the tabernacle, that the pillar of cloud descended and stood at the door of the tabernacle, and the LORD talked with Moses. All the people saw the pillar of cloud standing at the tabernacle door, and all the people rose and worshiped, each man in his tent door. So the LORD spoke to Moses face to face, as a man speaks to his friend. And he would return to the camp, but his servant Joshua the son of Nun, a young man, did not depart from the tabernacle. Then Moses said to the LORD, "See, You say to me, 'Bring up this people.' But You have not let me know whom You will send with me. Yet You have said, 'I know you by name, and you have also found grace in My sight.' Now therefore, I pray, if I have found grace in Your sight, show me now Your way, that I may know You and that I may find grace in Your sight. And consider that this nation is Your people." And He said, "My Presence will go with you, and I will give you rest." Then he said to Him, "If Your Presence does not go with us, do not bring us up from here." (Exodus 33:2-15)

C. **Acts 2** – Open heaven. God "rested" on 120 people in the upper room. This was an unprecedented number (the largest in history). This resting place was the culmination of the ministry of Christ himself. Jesus was more focused on a resting place with 120 than thousands following his teaching when he walked the earth. Christ was in touch with the centrality of the role of the manifest presence of the Spirit resting on a corporate people. He knew that 120 people living in an open heaven would result in more fruitfulness than gaining favor with the crowds in his earthly ministry.

D. Ananias and Saphira died because they lied to the Holy Spirit in the context of God's manifest presence (**Acts 5**). The greater the manifestation of God's glory - the greater the judgment on darkness. Great healing and glory was also released.

E. The End-Time prayer movement will release a consummation of David's vow. This will ultimately be fulfilled in the millennial kingdom followed by the new heavens and the new earth. God has saved the best wine for last. The dimension of power that is about to be released upon the church is unprecedented - beyond our current ability to comprehend. In the generation of the Lord's return, we will witness the miracles of the book of Exodus and the miracles of the book of Acts combined and multiplied on a global scale.

"And in the last days it shall be," God declares, "that I will pour out my Spirit on all flesh, and your sons and daughters shall prophesy, and your young men shall see visions, and your old men shall dream dreams…and I will show wonders in the heavens above and sign on the earth beneath, blood, and fire, and vapor of smoke…" (Acts 2:17-19)

And this gospel of the kingdom will be proclaimed throughout the whole world as a testimony [with power] to all nations, and then the end will come. (Matthew 24:14)

And I will grant authority to my two witnesses…they have the power to shut the sky, that no rain may fall during the days of their prophesying, and they have power of the waters to turn them into blood and to strike the earth with every kind of plague as often as they desire. (Revelation 11:6)

    1.   Currently, we are witnessing an unprecedented global prayer and missions movement. Many (if not most) missiologists believe that the great commission will be fulfilled in our generation.

2. Over 300 people have been resurrected from the dead in Mozambique in the last ten years!

3. The church is being restored in our generation.

IV. BUILDING THE RESTING PLACE: THE TABERNACLE OF DAVID

A. There is a very specific context in which the Lord will rest in fullness. David understood this principle. Towards this end, upon the establishment of his kingdom in Jerusalem, his first priority was to establish priestly ministry around the ark of the covenant. This is known as the "Tabernacle of David."

…my house shall be called a house of prayer…(Isaiah 56:7)

B. David hired 4,000 full-time musicians and 288 singers in order to facilitate the resting place. He also assigned 4,000 doorkeepers. This means there were 8,288 people designated to full-time ministry to the Lord through worship and intercession. This is known as the Tabernacle of David. Worship and ministry to the Lord is the central ingredient in building a resting place for the Lord.

These are the singers…who lodged in the chambers, and were free from other duties; for they were employed in that work day and night. (1Chronicles 9:33)

C. David spent about 100 billion dollars (according to today's value) to fund musicians and singers and the priestly ministry to the Lord during his reign.

D. David had a revelation of worship in the heavenly sanctuary (I Chron. 28:11-19).

I have seen the consummation of all perfection [God's Throne of Glory]…(Psalm 119:96)

David gave his son Solomon the plans… for all that he had by the Spirit, of the courts of the house of the LORD… also for the division of the priests and the Levites, for all the work of the service of the house of the LORD… "All this," said David, "the LORD made me understand in writing, by His hand upon me, all the works of these plans." (1 Chronicles 28:11-19)

E. The "Tabernacle of David" refers to both the Davidic dynasty and the day and night worship ministry, which was the centerpiece of David's rule. Prayer and worship is at the center of the government of heaven as it was in David's government.

F. When ministry to the Lord (worship/adoration) is our first priority, the resting place becomes a reality. In the West, ministry to people is often our greatest priority. However, our fruitfulness in ministry to people is minimized by not having a right priority of ministry to the Lord. Singing and music under the anointing of the Spirit brings us into agreement with God and results in a renewed mind and a context for power to be released. This is the wisdom of God.

G. The KJV says that God "inhabits" (lives in or manifests His life) the praises of his people.

You are...enthroned in the praises of Israel. (Psalm 22:3)

H. It is prayer and fasting that breaks through. It is ministry to the Lord that sustains a resting place. Azuza Street example:

The services ran almost continuously. Seeking souls could be found under the power almost any hour, night day. The place was never closed or empty. The people came to meet God. He was always there. Hence, the continuous meeting. The meeting did not depend on a human leader. God's presence became more and more wonderful. In the old building, with its low rafters and bare floors, God took strong men and women and to pieces, and put them together again, for his glory. Pride, self-assertion, self-importance, and self-esteem could not survive there...We saw some wonderful things in those days. (Guido Kuwas).

V.   PERFECT OBEDIENCE

I will behave wisely in a perfect way. Oh, when will You come to me?
I will walk within my house with a perfect heart. (Psalm 101:2)

A. In addition to sustained, corporate ministry to the Lord, there is specific heart reality that God looks for in which he will release his fullness. He waits for a people that are in total agreement and surrender.

B. God is striving against many of his people much of the time.

C. It is God's mercy that he does not give us the fullness of his manifest presence at this time. We must progress towards a visitation/habitation. We must prepare for his coming. This is the message of the forerunner (John the Baptist): <u>Obey now so that when he comes and the stakes go up, you will survive.</u>

D. This reality must be *fiercely* pursued. Once this vision gets in your heart, it will wound you and ruin you for anything less. It requires a lifestyle.

E. This vision will absolutely consume and cost everything. There is a stigma that is a God-given part of this pilgrimage into the fullness of God.

For it is for your sake that I have borne reproach, that dishonor has covered my face. I have become a stranger to my brothers, an alien to my mother's sons. <u>For zeal for your house has consumed me</u>, and the reproaches of those who reproach you have fallen on me. When I wept and humbled my soul with fasting, it became my reproach. When I made sackcloth my clothing, I became a byword to them. I am the talk of those who sit in the gate, and the drunkards make songs about me. (Psalm 69:7-12)

F. Before the end of the age, God will have a church that is in complete agreement with his heart and purposes. This will be expressed through a massive end-times prayer and worship movement and it will result in an explosion of power evangelism and, ultimately, the second coming of Jesus.

And the Spirit and the Bride say, 'Come!' (Revelation 22:17)

G. Consecration of this kind is best walked out in apostolic community. When the Spirit was poured out on the day of Pentecost, it was in the midst of unprecedented unity.

    1. Our mandate is to raise up an apostolic community that will embrace deep consecration and obedience, a spirit of prayer, and power evangelism. This community must be rooted in the urgency of the hour.

    2. Word to Corey Russell: *"You have not even seen the grace I am about to release for prayer, fasting, and consecration, <u>but you must do it in community</u>."*

    3. The reality of the resting place is only realized in the context of covenant community and authentic love for one another.

VI. DAVID'S VOW WILL BE EXPRESSED IN THE END-TIME WORSHIP MOVEMENT

A.   When the great harvest comes in, there will likely be more of God's people on earth than in heaven. In light of this, there will be more prayer for the release of the Kingdom on earth in the final years of natural history than all history combined.

B.   The Holy Spirit's End-Time prayer movement (Rev. 22:17; 5:8; 8:4; Lk. 18:7-8; Mt. 25:1-13; Isa. 62:6-7; 24:14-16; 25:9; 26:8-9; 27:2-5, 13; 30:18-19; 42:10-13; 43:26;51:11; 52:8; Joel 2:12-17, 32; Jer. 31:7; Mic. 5:3-4; Zeph. 2:1-3; Ps. 102:17-20; 122:6; Zech. 12:10, etc.)

C.   The End-Time worship movement will call Jesus to the earth at the time of the Second Coming. The Millennial worship movement will call the Father to the earth (Rev. 21:3).

   And the Spirit and the Bride say, 'Come!' (Revelation 22:17)

Session 4: The Past, Present, and the Future of the House of Prayer

I.   REVIEW

A.   Intercession is the calling of every believer. We are all priests in the New Covenant. Our priestly ministry is our first ministry from which all ministry to men derives its authority.

B.   From Genesis to Revelation, this is the central theme of the Bible. The operation, function, and release of the Kingdom of God is in conjunction with human involvement and intimacy. God created the image bearers, human beings, to partner with him in intimacy and dominion. God is the original and we are the counterpart. Through our union with him, we share his burdens and emotions and partner with him to rule the nations.

C.   God is looking for a priesthood with which he can fully share his heart and emotions. Priestly ministry (worship, intercession, intimacy, prophecy) is the context in which God will release his manifest glory on a global scale. God's intention is to rest with humans. He is building a dwelling place for himself by the Spirit.

II.   UNDERSTANDING THE TABERNACLE OF DAVID

A.   Around 1000 BC, King David commanded that the Ark of the Covenant be brought up on the shoulders of the Levites amidst the sound of songs and musical instruments to his new capital, Jerusalem. This command was the overflow of the passion of David's heart. There he had it placed in a tent and appointed two-hundred and eighty-eight prophetic singers and four thousand musicians to minister before the Lord, "to make petition, to give thanks and to praise the Lord" day and night (1 Chron. 15–17). This was unlike anything that had been done in Israel's history.

1. David was deemed by God as a man after his own heart (1 Sam. 13:14); the Lord chose him because he would display the heart and desire of God to dwell in the midst of Israel.

2. David was personally "eaten up" with zeal for the resting place of God with men.

   I will not enter my house or get into my bed, I will not give sleep to my eyes or slumber to my eyelids, until I find a place for the LORD a dwelling place for the Mighty One of Jacob (Psalm 132:3-5)

3. This ministry to the Lord in the tabernacle and the preparations for the temple cost David about *100 billion dollars* (according to today's numbers) of his personal finances.

B. The Tabernacle was a prophetic picture of the Messiah, the millennial reign and age to come. The actual Tabernacle was a fascinating place:

1. David brought the ark of the God back to Jerusalem, placed it in a tent and set singers and musicians around it day and night offering burnt sacrifices and offerings of worship and praise (1 Chron. 15-16).

2. Songs and poems were written before the ark as the priests stared into the glory and beauty of God. This is where we get the majority of the book of Psalms. There are few scriptures that so graphically express God's desire for intimacy and partnership with men as the Psalms (Ps. 2;8;22;24;27;29;45;50;84;110;139;149).

3. The Psalms are also some of the most significant Messianic prophecies in the Bible (e.g. Ps. 2, 110, 45, etc.). The musicians and singers in the tabernacle prophesied boldly. Worship, intercession, and prophecy are inseparable.

4. In contrast to Moses' tabernacle, the ark of the covenant was not behind a massive curtain, but it was open and surrounded by perpetual worship. This further speaks of God's desire to be encountered and our access to him in the New Covenant.

5.   The Tabernacle of David combined worship and intercession as the very heartbeat of Israel's culture and life. David was a cultural architect.

6.   The term "tabernacle" or "booth" of David also speaks of the Davidic dynasty, which is the messianic kingdom. This will be fully restored in the age to come.

C.   Interestingly, it is the tabernacle of David that God promised to rebuild and totally restore. This includes the Davidic dynasty and its central ministry of worship and intercession in the tabernacle. Amos prophesied this restoration in 750 B.C.

On that day I will raise up the tabernacle of David, which has fallen down, and repair its damages; I will raise up its ruins, and rebuild it as in the days of old (Amos 9:11)

1.   James quoted this passage at the first council of Jerusalem. He used this passage to frame the entire church age and the global missions expansion as an expression of the rebuilt tabernacle of David!

And after they had become silent, James answered, saying, "Men and brethren, listen to me: Simon has declared how God at the first visited the Gentiles to take out of them a people for His name. And with this the words of the prophets agree, just as it is written: "After this I will return and will rebuild the tabernacle of David, which has fallen down; I will rebuild its ruins, and I will set it up; So that the rest of mankind may seek the LORD, even all the Gentiles who are called by My name, says the LORD who does all these things." (Acts 15:13-17)

D.   Although the Tabernacle was replaced by a temple, the Davidic order of worship was embraced and reinstituted by six subsequent leaders in the history of Israel and Judah. Each time this order of worship was reintroduced, spiritual breakthrough, deliverance and military victory followed.

1.   Solomon instructed that worship in the temple should be in accordance with the Davidic Order *(2 Chronicles 8:14–15)*.

2. Jehoshaphat defeated Moab and Ammon by setting singers up in accordance with Davidic Order: singers at the front of the army singing the Great Hallel. Jehoshaphat reinstituted Davidic Worship in the temple *(2 Chronicles 20:20–22, 28)*.

3. Joash *(2 Chronicles 23–24:16-21)*

4. Hezekiah cleansed, re-consecrated and reinstituted the Davidic Order of worship in the temple *(2 Chronicles 29, 30:21)*.

5. Josiah reinstituted Davidic worship *(2 Chronicles 35)*.

6. Ezra and Nehemiah, returning from Babylon, reinstituted Davidic Worship *(Ezra 3:10, Nehemiah 12:28–47)*.

E. In May 1983, God spoke audibly to Bob Jones: "I will establish 24-hour prayer in the ***spirit of the tabernacle of David***." God is shifting the expression and understanding of Christianity globally in one generation. This shift is in the "spirit of the tabernacle of David."

F. So what was David's inspiration for this radical idea?

III. ON EARTH AS IT IS IN HEAVEN

A. After the disciples saw all the miracles and heard all of Christ's teaching, they came to Jesus with this one request, "Teach us to pray." Jesus replied by teaching them to pray for that which is modeled in heaven to be released on earth. At the very center of heavenly life is day and night worship and intercession.

And when he had taken the scroll, the four living creatures and the twenty-four elders fell down before the Lamb, each holding a harp, and golden bowls full of incense, which are the prayers of the saints. (Revelation 5:8)

1.   The eternal throne room is the governmental center of the universe. All things proceed from this throne room and from the One seated on the throne.

2.   The closest to the throne are four living creatures who "never cease day and night to say 'Holy, Holy, Holy is the Lord God Almighty, who was and is and is to come!'" This is their only logical response to what they are beholding.

3.   The harps speak of music and worship before the throne. The harp is the instrument that is associated with psalmody in the Old Testament. The harp is also regularly connected with prophecy more than any other instrument.

4.   The bowls of incense are the prayers of the saints. We must not think of the bowls as being "full" but continually being "filled to fullness" as the Body of Christ is anointed in prayer and is identified as a House of Prayer for all nations.

5.   Revelation 8 is a profound example of what happens when the union of worship and prayer rises before the throne. This is an end of the age prophecy, which is going to be fulfilled literally.

> *When the Lamb opened the seventh seal, there was silence in heaven for about half an hour. Then I saw the seven angels who stand before God, and seven trumpets were given to them. And another angel came and stood at the altar with a golden censer, and he was given much incense to offer with the prayers of all the saints on the golden altar before the throne, and the smoke of the incense, with the prayers of the saints, rose before God from the hand of the angel. Then the angel took the censer and filled it with fire from the altar and threw it on the earth, and there were peals of thunder, rumblings, flashes of lightning, and an earthquake. (Revelation 8:1-6)*

6.   Clearly in this passage God is releasing some of the most severe judgments (the trumpet judgments) on the earth at the end of the age

in response to these harps and bowls of incense. Our cries for justice and righteousness will be answered with a thunder from heaven.

7.   There is an altar before the throne that burns continuously with the fire of God.

> ***And the fire on the altar shall be kept burning on it; it shall not be put out. (Leviticus 6:12)***

IV.   MY HOUSE SHALL BE CALLED A HOUSE OF PRAYER FOR ALL NATIONS

And the foreigners who join themselves to the LORD, to minister to him, to love the name of the LORD, and to be his servants, everyone who keeps the Sabbath and does not profane it, and holds fast my covenant— these I will bring to my holy mountain, and make them joyful in my house of prayer; their burnt offerings and their sacrifices will be accepted on my altar; for my house shall be called a house of prayer for all peoples. (Isaiah 56:7)

A. Jesus quoted this passage in ***Matthew 21:12*** when he came into the temple and drove out the unjust business of buying and selling animals for sacrifice at an unjust price and exchanging money at a great profit. The disciples remembered that it was written, "zeal for your house has consumed me." (***Jn. 2:17; Ps. 69:9***)

B. Jesus is filled with the zeal of the Father for his house to be set apart only for encounter with himself unto adoration and intercession.

C. The great promise of Isaiah 56 is that he will *make* the gentiles joyful in the house of prayer. As we abide in this "house," our joy will invariably increase as we are swept up into heavenly realities and encounter the beauty of Jesus.

[2] In that day the Branch of the LORD shall be beautiful and glorious; (Isaiah 4: 2)

D. Before Jesus comes back, prayer will be at the center of the expression of the church globally. This is the great litmus test of the church at the end. It is the primary expression of faith that Jesus highlights in his teaching related to the victorious church at the end of the age.

The Spirit and the Bride say, "Come!" (Revelation 22:17)

And he told them a parable to the effect that they ought always to pray and not lose heart. He said, "In a certain city there was a judge who neither feared God nor respected man. And there was a widow in that city who kept coming to him and saying, 'Give me justice against my adversary.' For a while he refused, but afterward he said to himself, 'Though I neither fear God nor respect man, yet because this widow keeps bothering me, I will give her justice, so that she will not beat me down by her continual coming.'" And the Lord said, "Hear what the unrighteous judge says. And will not God give justice to his elect, who cry to him day and night? Will he delay long over them? I tell you, he will give justice to them speedily. <u>Nevertheless, when the Son of Man comes, will he find faith on earth?</u>" (Luke 18:1-7)

Many look forward to the second coming of Jesus – His coming again – as though mechanically, on a certain date, when certain events come to pass, Jesus is going to arrive. I do not see it that way. I see on the other hand that there must be a tremendous hunger, an overwhelming hunger, for the Lord's coming in the hearts of men, so that a prayer such as never was prayed in the world before for Christ to come rises to heaven. And, bless God, when it rises to heaven on the part of sufficient souls, it will take Jesus Christ himself off the throne and bring him down to earth. (John G. Lake)[8]

V.   TWO STRUCTURES

A.   Day and night prayer throughout history has left an indelible result of revival and cultural transformation.

B.   For over one thousand years, monasticism (a rhythm of life with a community of spiritual disciplines and prayer) held a central role in the practice of the church, the development of theology, and the transformation of societies. From as early as the fourth century, monks and nuns were an accepted part of culture and society. In spite of its many weaknesses and errors, monasticism was the most powerful missional force for the gospel for hundreds of years. Monasticism was the cradle which birthed *laus perennis*, or perpetual prayer.

---

[8] Lake, John G. *John G. Lake: The Complete Collection of His Life Teachings.* ed. Roberts Liardon. New Kensington: Whitaker House Pub., 1999. p. 453

C.   In order to understand the prayer movement, both historic and present day, it is critical that one understand the ecclesiology (study of the church) of the monastic/missions movements.

D.   There are ***two structures*** that are necessary to complete the Great Commission. These two structures have always been present throughout church history, though they have taken many distinct forms and expressions:

   1.   ***Apostolic structures ("sodalities")*** – This structure is focused on a specific missional/apostolic task. Examples of the sodalities are Paul's missions team, Jesus' team of disciples, monasteries, missions bases, city-wide ministries, universities, the Levitical priesthood, etc. Houses of prayer missions bases (as they are expressed in our context) are examples of this structure. They must be focused on an apostolic (God-given) assignment of day and night prayer and missions. They are, therefore, not ideal contexts for nurturing large communities of people over the long term. This structure, because of its intense nature, needs to be driven by teams of, essentially, full-time, vocational missionaries.

   2.   ***Local church structures ("modalities")*** – This structure is focused primarily on nurturing the body of Christ over the *long-term*. Though local congregations are very much still focused on the "assignment" of the great commission, their methodology is very different in that the overriding concern is for individuals to be pastored and nurtured over the long term. This is the "parish" or congregational structure.

E.   These two structures are inseparable from one another. There is a strong overlap between the two. For example, the sodality does nurture people, especially those who are related to their assignment specifically. And local congregations do move out in apostolic assignments. Sometimes, both structures work in one organization or ministry. But simply recognizing the differences helps make sense of the prayer movement. In order to accomplish certain apostolic assignments (e.g. day and night prayer), it is necessary to have an almost "unbalanced" focus on the assignment, but that is why we must have the whole picture of the Body of Christ to fulfill our mission.

VI.   BURNING AND SHINING LAMPS – DAY AND NIGHT PRAYER IN CHURCH HISTORY

   A.   **Alexander Akimites and the Sleepless Ones**

1. Alexander Akimites was an officer in the Roman Army that lived around 400 AD. Challenged by the words of Jesus to the rich young ruler in Matthew 19:21, he sold all his possessions and retreated from court life to the desert. He spent seven years in virtual solitude. While in the desert, he encountered a band of robbers whom he soundly converted to Christ – many of which became part of his subsequent monastic order. Shortly thereafter, he returned to Constantinople where he established a monastic order with about 300-400 monks.

2. Alexander's central priority in the monastic order was to establish *laus perennis* (perpetual prayer) to fulfill the Apostle Paul's exhortation to pray without ceasing (1 Thessalonians 5:17). Alexander divided the monks into six choirs, which rotated throughout the day to create uninterrupted worship and prayer twenty-four hours a day. He built a massive library and his order became, not only a house of prayer, but also one of the greatest learning centers in the world which was consulted by more than one pope. Alexander's practice of *laus perennis* soon passed into the Western church through another monk named St. Maurice of Agaune. In addition, Alexander's order developed the literal practice of Psalm 119:164: "Seven times a day I praise You..." This became an integral part of Benedictine rule with its seven hours of prayer —prime, tierce, sext, none, vespers, compline, matins, and lauds.

B. Comgall and Bangor:

1. In 433 AD, Patrick embarked on his famed missionary journey to evangelize the pagan peoples of Ireland (having been enslaved on the island previously, thereby gaining knowledge of the culture and language). Patrick was accompanied by a team of missionaries that were trained and influenced by the monasticism of Egypt and Constantinople. Since there were no urban centers in Ireland at the time, monasteries easily became cultural centers of the Irish nation. These monasteries all over Ireland embraced *laus perennis*. Ireland was praying day and night in the 400's AD!

2. At Bangor, Ireland, a man named Comgall instituted a rigid monastic rule of incessant prayer and fasting. Far from turning people away, this ascetic rule attracted thousands. Comgall had about 3,000 monks in his community at the time of his death.

3. The location of Bangor found its first significance on Patrick's earlier missionary journeys in Ireland. Patrick and his comrades happened upon the valley of Bangor where they experienced a "vision of heaven." They

saw the "valley filled with heavenly light, and with a multitude of heaven, they heard, as chanted forth from the voice of angels, the psalmody of the celestial choir." The great Bangor prayer and missions movement began its life here.

4. The monks of Bangor carried out the practice of *laus perennis* with vigor and passion, even beyond Alexander Akimites. They organized antiphonal choirs and embraced "perpetual psalmody." This extravagant worship and prayer went unbroken day and night for over 250 years!

5. The Celtic monks were instrumental in re-evangelizing Western Europe and preserving Western literature and culture after the fall of Rome. Bangor became one of the most renowned centers of education in Europe. It was one of the greatest missions movements in the history of the church. Thomas Cahill wrote a famous book about these Celtic monks called *How the Irish Saved Civilization*.

C. **Cluny:**

1. In the ninth and tenth century, the monastic movement was shaken as Viking invaders were shifting the culture of European towards an increasingly violent norm. Feudalism was taking root in Western Civilization. As a result of this upheaval, arguably one of the greatest reform movements in the Western church began. The Cluniac Order embodied this movement. The monastery at Cluny was founded by William the Pious in 910 AD. This monastic order was known to be even stricter than the Benedictine Order and was focused on day and night prayer as its central reality. In fact, the Cluniac Order, which by the twelfth century included more than 314 monasteries across the continent of Europe, actually replaced much of Benedictine manual labor with increased hours of prayer and worship.

D. **Count Zinzendorf and the Moravians:**

1. The next historical champion of day and night prayer did not appear until the beginning of the eighteenth century. The Holy Spirit apprehended a German Count named Count Ludwig Von Zinzendorf at a young age. While attending a Pietist school as a young man, he formed a club called the "Honorable Order of the Mustard Seed." This "order" was committed to a lifestyle of consecration and wholehearted love for God. Zinzendorf was true to this commitment for the rest of his life.

2. In 1722, Zinzendorf bought the Berthelsdorf estate from his grandmother. That same year, Zinzendorf met a leader of the persecuted protestants of Moravia. These Moravians were followers of John Huss who had been persecuted for centuries under repressive Catholic monarchies. Zinzendorf invited them to his land for refuge. Thus began the Moravian community of Herrnhut, which means, "watch of the Lord."

3. In 1726, the community of Herrnhut was filled with division and strife based on various doctrinal disagreements. Zinzendorf was zealous that the community not dissolve in discord. He began to go door to door and ask the community to join him in the place of prayer recognizing that they had Christ in common. The response was a historic event in August of 1727 known as the "Moravian Pentecost." Zinzendorf said that August 13th "was a day of the outpourings of the Holy Spirit upon the congregation; it was its Pentecost." Within two weeks of this significant outpouring, various members of the Moravian community committed to pray day and night in hourly intercessions. Their commitment was that the "fire on the altar should never go out" (Lev. 6:13). This prayer meeting lasted twenty-four hours per day in Herrnhut for over 100 years.

4. This 100-year prayer meeting birthed one of the greatest missions movements in history. With a matter of years, the Moravians were selling themselves into slavery to go America and reach the African slaves for Christ. Over 226 missionaries came out of the Herrnhut community filled with zeal for the gospel. The great cry of the Moravian missions movement was, "May the Lamb receive the reward of His suffering!" William Carey, who is known as the "father of modern missions" said that Zinzendorf and the Moravians were a significant source of his inspiration.

5. John Wesley, the great revivalist of the 18th century and one of the primary leaders of the first great awakening, was converted to Christ after an encounter with the Moravians. In fact, many believe that the Moravians' prayer meeting and missions movement was the catalyst for the first great awakening in Europe and America in the 1730s and 40s.

VII. 24/7 PRAYER IN THE 20TH CENTURY

A. Welsh Revival

1.   In 1904, a man, Evan Roberts, after crying out in prayer for revival for almost 11 years, had a spiritual experience which would lead him back to the young people of his own church, Moriah Loughor, where he shared his experience and encouraged them to be open to God's Spirit.

2.   Meetings that broke the conventional and bi-passed the traditional began. Often the ministers just sat down unable to preach or understand what storm had arrived in their normally sedate temples.

3.   This outpouring led to cultural transformation. The crime rate dropped, drunkards were reformed, pubs were transformed into churches. Bad language disappeared and never returned to the lips of many. It was reported that the pit ponies failed to understand their born again colliers who seemed to speak the new language of Zion – without curse and blasphemy. Even football and rugby became uninteresting in the light of new joy and direction received by the converts.

4.   Over 150,000 souls were saved in the first 6 months.

5.   The revival fires burning in Wales in 1904-05 spread through England, Ireland, and Scotland. Prayer meetings multiplied. As many as 2,000 people attended a prayer meeting in the city of Bradford. In the city of Leeds, Samuel Chadwick reported that his church was never empty all day. An amazing work of grace transformed life in a factory.

B. Azusa Street

1.   Frank Bartleman wrote Evan Roberts to get instructions on how to experience a move of God in Los Angeles. Roberts wrote back, "Congregate the people who are willing to make a total surrender. Pray and wait. Believe God's promises. Hold daily meetings. May God bless you is my earnest prayer."

2.   William Seymour, who was a one-eyed African America man, became gripped with the cry for the baptism of the Holy Spirit when he would sit outside of Charles Parham's classes in Houston, TX. He moved and joined Bartleman in Los Angles, CA where he began to preach the need for the baptism of the Holy Spirit. He was kicked out of churches and shunned for this "new" belief.

3.   Seymour began His ministry with a prayer group that had been meeting regularly at the home of Richard and Ruth Asbery at 214 North Bonnie Brae Street.

4.   As the group sought God for revival, their hunger intensified, and they embraced extended corporate fasting for the baptism of the Holy Spirit. This included prayer that would frequently last all night. A powerful outpouring followed which began at a 2 AM prayer meeting. Many received the Holy Spirit baptism as Pentecostal revival arrived on the West Coast. That evening would be hard to describe. People fell to the floor as if unconscious; others shouted and ran through the house. One neighbor, Jennie Evans Moore, played the piano, something she did not have the ability to do before being filled with the Holy Spirit.

5.   Over the next few days of continuous outpouring, hundreds gathered. The streets were filled and Seymour preached from the Asbery's porch. On April 12, three days after the initial outpouring, Seymour received his baptism of power. Quickly outgrowing the Asbery home, the faithful searched for a home for a new church. They found their building at 312 Azusa Street. For about three years, the glory of God filled the gatherings in this humble building to such a degree that a literal cloud filled the room nightly. The fire department was called on multiple occasions as the building appeared, from the outside, to be on fire.

6.   Thousands were saved, healed, and delivered. From this outpouring, we have the Pentecostal Movement and the gifts of the Spirit beginning to be restored to the Body of Christ.

C. South Korea set ablaze.

1.   In 1973, David Yonggi Cho, Pastor of the Yoido Full Gospel Church in Seoul, South Korea, established a Prayer Mountain in night and day prayer. The Prayer Mountain was soon attracting over a million visitors per year, as people would spend retreats in the prayer cells provided on the mountain. Cho had a commitment to continuous prayer, to faith, and to establishing small discipleship cells in his church. Perhaps as a result, Cho's church rapidly expanded to become the largest church congregation on the globe, with membership now over 780,000.

D. Global Day of Prayer

1.   The Global Day of Prayer began in South Africa in 2000. Every year since, an estimated 250 million believers gathered on Pentecost Sunday to call on the name of the Lord for global harvest and justice and in the nations. This is the largest prayer meeting in church history.

E. International House of Prayer and 24/7 Prayer Movement

1.   On September 19, 1999, the International House of Prayer in Kansas City, Missouri, started a prayer and worship meeting that has continued for twenty-four hours a day, seven days a week ever since. With a similar vision to Zinzendorf, that the fire on the altar should never go out, there has never been a time when worship and prayer has not ascended to Heaven since that date. At the same time, a movement of day and night prayer broke out across Europe and the nations.

VIII. END-TIME PRAYER AND WORSHIP MOVEMENT

A.   The Holy Spirit's End-Time movement (Rev. 22:17; 5:8; 8:4; Lk. 18:7-8; Mt. 25:1-13; Isa. 62:6- 7; 24:14-16; 25:9; 26:8-9; 27:2-5, 13; 30:18-19; 42:10-13; 43:26;51:11; 52:8; Joel 2:12-17, 32; Jer. 31:7; Mic. 5:3-4; Zeph. 2:1-3; Ps. 102:17-20; 122:6; Zech. 12:10, etc.)

B.   The judgments of the Book of Revelation will not happen to the church but through the praying church, even as the plagues of Egypt happened through Moses. We will participate with the Holy Spirit in revival, judgment, and the return of Jesus.

C.   The End-Time worship movement will call Jesus to the earth at the time of the Second Coming. The Millennial worship movement will call the Father to the earth (Rev. 21:3).

The Spirit and the Bride say, "Come!" (Revelation 22:17)

Therefore, holy brethren, partakers of a heavenly calling, <u>consider Jesus, the Apostle and High Priest</u> of our calling. (Hebrews 3:1)

And it is yet far more evident if, in the likeness of Melchizedek, <u>there arises another priest</u> who has come, not according to the law of a fleshly commandment, but <u>according to the power of an endless life.</u> For He testifies: "You are a priest forever according to the order of Melchizedek." (Hebrews 7:15-17)

I.   THE ARM OF THE LORD REVEALED

Then the LORD saw it, and it displeased Him that there was no justice. He saw that there was no man, and wondered that there was no intercessor; therefore His own arm brought salvation for Him; And His own righteousness, it sustained Him. (Isaiah 59:15-16)

A.   For all of history, God has sought for a people with whom he could fully share his heart, his thoughts, and his emotions. He searched for an intercessor and found no one on earth. No one could fully identify with God's holiness and with man's sinfulness. This is the essence of priestly ministry: to be fully one with God and to fully identify with man. God's intention from creation is that we, as image bearers, function in this role of intimacy and intercession.

B.   The Lord was grieved that he could find no one to save his image bearers (humans). The Lord was filled with deep love for humans and deep hatred for sin that destroys his creation. He longed for someone to stand in the whirlwind of God's justice and mercy and triumph over death and sin.

C.   Finally, the Lord became our salvation and revealed his arm (power) to the earth. He became our great high priest. He became our intercessor. Jesus Christ is fully God and man. He fully indentified with God's nature and fully with man's weakness. He bore our sin and the wrath of God for us. He went to hell for three days. He rose again from the dead, triumphing over hell and the grave forever. He ascended to heaven and now he is at the right hand of the Father always interceding for us. Soon, he will return to fully manifest his victory over sin, sickness, and Satan. This is the ultimate priestly ministry.

D.   God reaches towards man, and man reaches towards God, and they finally collide in the Person and work of Christ Jesus, our Great High Priest.

E. Our heavenly High Priest is sympathetic to our human weakness. I remember the first time I realized that Jesus is filled with sympathy and compassion for me on a personal level. We have an advocate at the throne of grace. There is a man standing at the right hand of the Father that is filled with sympathy for us. Furthermore, he ever lives to intercede for us.

Seeing then that we have a great High Priest who has passed through the heavens, Jesus the Son of God, let us hold fast our confession. For we do not have a High Priest who cannot sympathize with our weaknesses, but was in all points tempted as we are, yet without sin. Let us therefore come boldly to the throne of grace that we may obtain mercy and find grace to help in time of need. (Hebrews 4:14-16)

II. THE DAZZLING PERSON

A. Christ is the beginning and end of God's sovereign story of redemption and intimacy with humans. He is our exceedingly great reward. In God's plan, we are his inheritance and he is our inheritance.

Yet indeed I also count all things loss for the excellence of the knowledge of Christ Jesus my Lord, for whom I have suffered the loss of all things, and count them as rubbish, that I may gain Christ and be found in Him, not having my own righteousness, which is from the law, but that which is through faith in Christ, the righteousness which is from God by faith; that I may know Him and the power of His resurrection, and the fellowship of His sufferings, being conformed to His death, if, by any means, I may attain to the resurrection from the dead. (Philippians 3:8-11)

B. We were created with an insatiable desire for pleasure. This is not something from which we can repent. Our very reason for existence is to experience the glorious splendor of God intimately forever. Thereby, we glorify God. The highest revelation of God to the human race is Christ Jesus and our oneness with him. He is the great prophetic word that the human race is searching for.

God, who at various times and in various ways spoke in time past to the fathers by the prophets, has in these last days spoken to us by His Son, whom He has appointed heir of all things, through whom also He made the worlds; who being the brightness of His glory and the express image of His person, and upholding all things by the word of His power, when He had by Himself purged our sins, sat down at the right hand of the Majesty on high, having become so much better than the angels, as He has by inheritance obtained a more excellent name than they. (Hebrews 1:1-4)

C.   I am convinced that the greatest crisis in this nation is a lack of the true, personal knowledge of the Son of God in and through the church. Our pulpits have been filled with self-help strategies, humanism, and a man-centered gospel. The key to end-time revival is the revelation of the glory of God in the face of Christ and an intimate knowledge of him.

D.   Paul was wise when he chose to know *nothing* except Jesus Christ and him crucified.

For I resolved to know nothing (to be acquainted with nothing, to make a display of the knowledge of nothing, and to be conscious of nothing) among you except Jesus Christ (the Messiah) and Him crucified. (1 Corinthians 2:2 amplified)

E.   The single most contested issue at the end of the age will be the identity of Jesus and his unique claims.

For many will come in My name, saying, "I am the Christ," and will deceive many. (Matthew 24:5)

F.   The Holy Spirit is orchestrating a movement of love in the hearts of humans from every nation, of which Jesus is worthy. This is the Holy Spirit's primary function right now in the nations of the earth. We will love Jesus the way that the Father loves Jesus.

And I have declared to them Your name, and will declare it, that the love with which You loved Me may be in them, and I in them. (John 17:26)

G.   This is the primary purpose of the prayer and worship movement. When we think of prayer and worship, we should think of a Person. Otherwise, our prayer and worship is reduced to forms and dominated by an overwhelming concern for the outward shape that it takes.

In that day the Branch of the LORD shall be beautiful and glorious (Isaiah 4:2)

H.   Evaluate this statement: "That worship was good."

I.   Many people are perplexed by that idea of day and night worship. Interestingly, the idea of day and night Wal-Mart, McDonalds, or a fitness gym is not equally perplexing to them. When we encounter the splendor of the person and work of Christ Jesus, incessant adoration is the only logical response. The reason for the absence of prayer and worship in our communities, and for all the objections against it, is the lack of revelation of the glory of God in the face of Christ!

J.   Everything is going to be summed up in the Person of Christ. He is the beginning and end of all things!

> *…that in the dispensation of the fullness of the times He might gather together in one all things in Christ, both which are in heaven and which are on earth—in Him. (Ephesians 1:10)*

III.   HIS WORK IS BEAUTIFUL

A.   *Christology:* the study of the person and work of Christ. This is absolutely, categorically the foundation of day and night prayer, worship, and missions.

B.   Pre-existence

1.   Jesus is the second person of the Trinity. The Trinity is three Persons with the same essence. They are fully One. Jesus is uncreated. There was never a time when he did not exist. He is equally present at every moment of human history as fully God.

> *And now, O Father, glorify Me together with Yourself, with the glory which I had with You before the world was. (John 17:5)*

2.   Jesus, the second Person of the Trinity, personally created all that exists. Indeed, everything was made *for* him.

> *For by Him all things were created that are in heaven and that are on earth, visible and invisible, whether thrones or dominions or principalities or powers. All things were created through Him and for Him. (Colossians 1:16)*

C.   Incarnation

1. The incarnation was that unfathomable moment when the uncreated God became a human embryo in the womb of Mary. He is both fully God and fully human.

   Jesus said to them, "Most assuredly, I say to you, before Abraham was, I AM." (John 8:58)

2. Jesus was truly human – with a personality, emotions, and opinions – all of which perfectly reveal the Father to us. He fully sympathizes with human weakness.

   For you know the grace of our Lord Jesus Christ, that though He was rich, yet for your sakes He became poor, that you through His poverty might become rich. (2 Corintians 8:9)

3. In the eternal councils of God, Jesus considered the human beings and the human body so highly that he was willing to have a human body forever!

D. Life and Death

1. Jesus lived as a demonstration of perfect humanity. He *grew* in wisdom. Even his miracles were performed through the power of the Spirit.

2. Jesus' work of atonement through his death and resurrection was the most shocking and pivotal moment in history. He took us to the grave with him. He bore all the wrath of God for us. Nothing was held back.

   Now this, "He ascended" — what does it mean but that He also first descended into the lower parts of the earth? He who descended is also the One who ascended far above all the heavens, that He might fill all things. (Ephesians 4:9-10)

   Lord God, Joy of the heavenly court, how could you – as if you were the most foolish of men – allow yourself to be thus mocked, spat upon, and struck by such vile men? Your tormentors, filled with fury, spent that entire night beating and ridiculing you, and by the time they had their fill of punishing you, your face was hardly recognizable. Through all this you maintained an incomparable meekness and matchless modesty of soul that your wicked tormentors were incapable of perceiving. Because you were innocent you suffered all these things out of love and, therefore, you have become dearer and more lovable to all the elect, who, following the interior motions of their soul, acknowledge you as their Supreme Good. (Thomas a Kempis)

I have been crucified with Christ; it is no longer I who live, but Christ lives in me; and the life which I now live in the flesh I live by faith in the Son of God, who loved me and gave Himself for me. (Galatians 2:20)

3. Jesus expressed his motive on the cross in his final prayer for church before the cross:

Father, I desire that they also whom You gave Me may be with Me where I am, that they may behold My glory which You have given Me; for You loved Me before the foundation of the world. (John 17:24)

He (the Father) *so loved the world that he seemed for a time not to love his Son in comparison of it, or equal with it. God valued our redemption above the worldly happiness of the Redeemer, and sentenced him to an humiliation on the earth in order to order our exaltation in heaven. He was desirous to hear him groaning, and see him bleeding, that we might not groan under his frowns, and bleed under his wrath; He spared him not, that he might spare us; refused not to strike him that he may be well-pleased with us...he was willing to have the Son made man, and die, rather than man should perish, who had delighted to ruin himself.*[9]

E. Resurrection, Ascension, Session

1. Jesus' resurrection was our resurrection.

For if we have been united together in the likeness of His death, certainly we also shall be in the likeness of His resurrection. (Romans 6:5)

2. Jesus' resurrection is our only hope. He is alive. The evidence of his resurrection as a proven fact is truly overwhelming. Literally hundreds of people claimed to have personally seen him after his resurrection. At least

---

[9] Charnock, Stephen. *The Existence and Attributes of God.* Grand Rapids, MI; Baker Books, 1996, p. 264.

500 people at one time saw him, and he taught them in his resurrected body. Many of these, including all but one of his 12 apostles, died gruesome deaths for this belief in the resurrection of Jesus.

3.   Jesus, as a resurrected man, is the perfection of humanity. He is dazzlingly beautiful in all his attributes.

My beloved is dazzling and ruddy, outstanding among ten thousand. (Song of Solomon 5:10)

4.   Jesus' ascension was our ascension.

and raised us up together, and made us sit together in the heavenly places in Christ Jesus (Ephesians 2:6)

5.   His session is our session (intercession).

Therefore He is also able to save to the uttermost those who come to God through Him, since He always lives to make intercession for them. (Hebrews 7:25)

F.   Second Coming

Be sober, and rest your hope fully upon the grace that is to be brought to you at the revelation of Jesus Christ [second coming]. (1 Peter 1:13)

1.   The Holy Spirit will emphasize *3 facets of the beauty of Jesus*, as clearly seen in Scriptures, that describe God's End-Time plans (**Rev. 19; Mt. 24-25; Isa. 60-62**). There will be no contradiction in Jesus' heart and ministry as He manifests His glory as a Bridegroom, King, and Judge. He does not suspend one attribute to exercise another:

a.   Jesus as a *passionate Bridegroom*: has great tenderness and deep desire for His people.

b.   Jesus as a *powerful King*: releases power in confronting darkness and winning the lost. He will literally take over every earthly government.

    c.   Jesus as a ***righteous Judge***: upholds the standards of conduct (holiness).

IV.   THE PRIESTLY ORDER OF MELCHIZEDEK

A.   The priesthood of Jesus Christ is after the order of Melchizedek. He is a priest *forever*. The Melchizedek priesthood is far superior to the Aaronic and Levitical Priesthood. The sons of Aaron and the sons of Levi were but types and shadows of the greater priesthood, which is in the order of Melchizedek. Our priesthood is also after Melchizedek, as we are being conformed to the image of Jesus.

B.   We are part of the Melchizedek priesthood because our priestly ministry is through regeneration and the power of the Spirit within us. Our priestly ministry is far superior to the old covenant.

C.   Melchizedek is first mentioned in Genesis 14. There are only three short verses about this Priest-King in Genesis, which was a reflection of the priestly/kingly ministry of Christ Jesus.

> ***Then Melchizedek king of Salem brought out bread and wine; he was the priest of God Most High. And he blessed him and said: "Blessed be Abram of God Most High, possessor of heaven and earth. And blessed be God Most High, who has delivered your enemies into your hand." And he gave him a tithe of all. (Genesis 14:18-20)***

D.   "He was a priest of God Most High" (Gen. 14:18)

    1.   Melchizedek was not a priest based on family (natural, human descent). His priesthood is eternal, even as God is eternal. It is not based on temporal realities. Some believe this implies that this is actually a pre-incarnate appearance of Jesus. This is certainly a likely possibility. At the very least, Melchizedek was the clearest picture of the priestly ministry of Jesus in the Old Testament.

> *...without father, without mother, without genealogy, having neither beginning of days nor end of life, but made like the Son of God, remains a priest continually. (Hebrews 7:3)*

2.   Jesus, like Melchizedek, is a priest forever by the *power of an indestructible life*. He is a priest by the power of the life of God dwelling within him. Our priestly ministry is after this same order. God gives us a new spirit, and therefore a priestly calling. The priestly ministry of Melchizedek is utterly divine in origin. It is not based in any way on natural abilities. In fact, all natural abilities (the old man) die with Christ.

> *"The Melchizedek order is above culture, time, and nationality. It is without beginning of days or ending of life. In fact, anything earthly contradicts it. The Aaronic priesthood required genealogy, ancestry, and earthly identification. The new resembles the Son of God, a priest without interruption and who abides eternally... What kind of priesthood is this? ...It is to be performed in a continual flow, out of the throne of God Himself, on the basis of the power of an endless and indestructible life."* [10]

> *"You are in the Melchizedek priesthood in exact proportion as you are abiding in the Son, no more and no less. It has nothing to do with natural factors, but only with resurrection life, a life offered in sacrifice and raised up in glory. We are brought to a transcendent place of identification with Him by which every natural, racial, religious, ethnic, and other distinction is transcended."* [11]

3.   Jesus is the "only begotten" of the Father. He is the first-born among many brothers. His priestly ministry flows from his sonship. The priestly ministry of Melchizedek was literally born from above, while later priestly orders where begotten of their parents under sin.

> **So also Christ did not exalt himself to be made a high priest, but was appointed by him who said to him, "You are my Son, today I have begotten you;" as he says also in another place, "You are a priest forever after the order of Melchizedek." (Hebrews 5:5-6)**

4.   Melchizedek's (Christ's) ministry was essentially heavenly. Even while on earth Jesus was "in heaven". He literally ascended into heaven where he is now functioning in his priestly calling. Christ ascended into the heavenly temple as an advocate for all who call on his name. His ascension is our ascension. We now have bold access to the very throne of the Father through Jesus.

---

[10] Katz, Art. *Apostolic Foundations.* Laporte, MN: Burning Bush Pub, 1999. p. 48.

[11] *Ibid.* p. 50.

No one has ascended to heaven but He who came down from heaven, that is, the Son of Man who is in heaven. (John 3:13)

Seeing then that we have a great High Priest who has passed through the heavens, Jesus the Son of God, let us hold fast our confession. For we do not have a High Priest who cannot sympathize with our weaknesses, but was in all points tempted as we are, yet without sin. Let us therefore come boldly to the throne of grace, that we may obtain mercy and find grace to help in time of need. (Hebrews 4:14-16)

For if He were on earth, He would not be a priest, since there are priests who offer the gifts according to the law (Hebrews 8:4)

E.   "Melchizedek, king of Salem" (Gen. 14:18)

1.   Melchizedek was a king and a priest. This was unheard of in the Aaronic and Levitical priesthood. He was literally king of Salem (Jerusalem), which means "peace." Melchizedek's very nature brought peace to Abraham. He carries an impartation of peace to those who receive his priestly ministry. Jesus is the "Prince of Peace." Ultimately, the result will be peace in all the nations of the earth. There is none more pleasant or peaceful than Christ.

And His name will be called...Prince of Peace. Of the increase of His government and peace, there will be no end (Isaiah 9:6-7)

And the God of peace will crush Satan under your feet shortly. The grace of our Lord Jesus Christ be with you. Amen. (Romans 16:20)

2.   God has forever joined the kingly ministry to the priestly ministries of intimacy, intercession, and servanthood. This is the only pathway to greatness and authority in the Kingdom of God. We are a kingdom of priests, led by a King-Priest.

...and he will be a priest on his throne... (Zechariah 6:13)

F.   "[Melchizedek] brought out bread and wine....he blessed him [Abraham]..." (Gen. 14:18-19) - THE CROSS

And as they were eating, Jesus took bread, blessed and broke it, and gave it to the disciples and said, "Take, eat; this is My body." Then He took the cup, and gave thanks, and gave it to them, saying, "Drink from it, all of you. For this is My blood of the new covenant, which is shed for many for the remission of sins." (Matthew 26:26)

1. The ultimate expression of priestly ministry is the cross. Jesus is not only our Great High Priest, but also the sacrifice for our eternal redemption. His very body and blood is our food and drink, which gives eternal life. He blessed us at the greatest cost. Now we have an eternal feast of his own Person!

2. The old order of priesthood was required to make repeated sacrifices because the priests and the sacrifices were imperfect. Jesus was the perfect sacrifice himself, and since he rose from the dead, his sacrifice remains forever. It is eternally finished. He has conquered death forever. He is at the right hand of the Father. No other sacrifices will ever be necessary.

    For such a High Priest was fitting for us, who is holy, harmless, undefiled, separate from sinners, and has become higher than the heavens; who does not need daily, as those high priests, to offer up sacrifices, first for His own sins and then for the people's, for this He did once for all when He offered up Himself. For the law appoints as high priests men who have weakness, but the word of the oath, which came after the law, appoints the Son who has been perfected forever. (Hebrews 7:26-28)

3. All the attributes of God are displayed on the cross. We will spend all of eternity meditating on the majestic splendor of Jesus as our Great High Priest on the cross. He became sin for us.

4. *"The strong cries of Jesus could not cause him to cut off the least fringe of this royal garment. The torrent of wrath is opened upon him, and the Father's heart beats not in the least notice of tenderness to sin, in the midst of His Son's agonies. God seems to lay aside the bowels of a father, and put on the garb of an irreconcilable enemy. He seems to hang upon the cross like a disinherited son, while he appeared in the rank and garb of a sinner."[12]*

---

[12] Charnock, Stephen. *The Existence and Attributes of God* (Grand Rapids, MI: Baker Books, 1996). p. 136

5.   Jesus had one great motivation in his death on the cross: desire.

Father, I desire that those whom you gave Me may be with Me where I am, that they may behold My glory which You have given Me; for You have loved Me from before the foundation of the world. (John 17:24)

6.   The cross opened the banqueting table of the joy of the Lord to us. He served us bread and wine. The finished work of the cross purchased joy, pleasure, power, and fullness beyond our wildest dreams.

7.   Even in the cross, we are being conformed to the image of Jesus. We died with him, and we are experiencing his sufferings and his death to all that is our flesh in this age, that we may be glorified with him. This is the only way to experience the glory of God: complete death to self that life may flow.

Then Jesus said to His disciples, "If anyone desires to come after Me, let him deny himself, and take up his cross, and follow Me." (Matthew 16:24)

G.   "And he [Abraham] gave him a tithe of everything" (Gen. 14:20)

1.   Abraham, the man of faith, recognized Melchizedek as his superior and, therefore, gave him a tenth of all his possessions. This is the first tithe to a priest. This is the only fitting response, to give of ourselves radically. The priestly ministry Jesus demands is this kind of extravagant response. There is no record that Melchizedek ever required this of Abraham. It was the spontaneous overflow of his heart.

2.   This demonstrated that Melchizedek was greater than any other priesthood, because all the other priests were still in the "loins" of Abraham.

Now consider how great this man was, to whom even the patriarch Abraham gave a tenth of the spoils. And indeed those who are of the sons of Levi, who receive the priesthood, have a commandment to receive tithes from the people according to the law, that is, from their brethren, though they have come from the loins of Abraham; but he whose genealogy is not derived from them received tithes from Abraham and blessed him who had the promises. Now beyond all contradiction the lesser is blessed by the better. Here mortal men receive tithes, but there he receives them, of whom it is witnessed that he lives. Even Levi, who receives tithes, paid tithes through Abraham, so to speak, for he was still in the loins of his father when Melchizedek met him. (Hebrews 7:4-10)

V.   IDENTIFICATION

A.   It is important to note the principle of identification. By faith, we are fully one with Christ in his complete work as co-heirs with him (Gal. 2:20; Eph. 2:5; Rom. 6:8; Eph.2:6).

B.   The phrase "in Christ" is used 90 times in the NT. Knowing the fullness of what Jesus has accomplished for us is central to our growth in our priestly ministry.

Likewise you also, reckon yourselves to be dead indeed to sin, but alive to God in Christ Jesus our Lord. (Romans 6:11)

...nor height nor depth, nor any other created thing, shall be able to separate us from the love of God which is in Christ Jesus our Lord. (Romans 8:39)

Therefore I have reason to glory in Christ Jesus in the things which pertain to God. (Romans 15:17)

For as in Adam all die, even so in Christ all shall be made alive. (1 Corinthians 15:22)

Now thanks be to God who always leads us in triumph in Christ, and through us diffuses the fragrance of His knowledge in every place. (2 Corinthians 2:14)

...that in the dispensation of the fullness of the times He might gather together in one all things in Christ, both which are in heaven and which are on earth— in Him. (Ephesians 1:10)

and raised us up together, and made us sit together in the heavenly places in Christ Jesus (Ephesians 2:6)

Session 6: Walking in the Spirit

I.   NEW CREATIONS

For I resolved to know nothing (to be acquainted with nothing, to make a display of the knowledge of nothing, and to be conscious of nothing) among you except Jesus Christ (the Messiah) and Him crucified. (1 Corinthians 2:2 amplified)

A.   Most believers are not aware of the fullness of what the atoning work of Jesus accomplished for them. This is the great Pauline burden that Christ and him crucified would be known and proclaimed with boldness. The cross is far more outrageous, exhilarating, and extravagant than we can comprehend. Most of the primary apostolic prayers of the New Testament are for the church to comprehend the splendor of Jesus and what he has done in us.

B.   Through faith in Jesus Christ, we have been given a fundamentally new nature. We are new creations. The Greek word for "creation" actually means "creature" or "species." When we are born again, we receive a new nature of righteousness. We are not bound to a sin nature anymore.

If anyone is in Christ, he is a <u>new creation</u>; old things have passed away...<u>all things have become new</u>... that we might <u>become the righteousness</u> of God. (2 Corinthians 5:17-21)

C.   In order to understand the glory of the new creation reality, we must understand how God created human beings. We are made of three parts: body, soul, and spirit. Our soul is our mind, our will, and our emotions. When we are born again, we are given a new spirit. Our spirit is recreated and made alive in God. You will never be more righteous than you are right now in your spirit. We have been resurrected with Christ!

Now may the God of peace Himself sanctify you completely; and may your whole <u>spirit, soul, and body</u> be preserved blameless at the coming of our Lord Jesus Christ. (1 Thessalonians 5:23)

1.   We are saved in our spirit at our new birth (salvation). This is our true identity.

2. We are being saved in our soul (sanctification). This is just as much through the high priestly work of Jesus. Sanctification is simply the fuller experience of our new creation in Christ.

3. We will be saved in our body (glorification/resurrected bodies).

D. Furthermore, when we are joined to the Lord (born again), the Holy Spirit comes to live in our spirit, and we are made to be one spirit with him. Right now, you have all nine fruits of the Spirit and all nine gifts of the Spirit living in your spirit. Our process of sanctification is simply learning to access and live out of the life of God within us. Most believers do not know who they are in their spirit and live far below their inheritance.

But he who is joined to the Lord is one spirit with Him. (1 Corinthians 6:21)

E. The Apostle Paul outlines two orientations of the mind and soul, which have very different results. It is possible to live disconnected from the realities of our new nature and the indwelling Spirit, which is the reason for such powerlessness in the Body of Christ. We must learn to fellowship with the Spirit and access his power and life.

Do not walk according to the flesh but according to the Spirit. Those who live according to the flesh set their minds on the things of the flesh, but those who live according to the Spirit, the things of the Spirit. (Romans 8:4-5)

F. It is critical that we think rightly about ourselves. Through our new nature, we have died to sin. We are no longer under the dominion of the old nature. We can "reign in grace" over sin. We are to think of ourselves as alive in God.

Reckon [see] yourselves to be...alive to God in Christ... (Romans 6:11)

II. THE RENEWED MIND

And do not be conformed to this world, but be transformed by the renewing of your mind, that you may prove what is that good and acceptable and perfect will of God. (Romans 12:2)

But we all, with unveiled face, <u>beholding as in a mirror</u> the glory of the Lord, are being <u>transformed into the same image from glory to glory</u>, just as <u>by the Spirit of the Lord</u>. (2 Corinthains 3:18)

A.   The renewed mind is the key to life in the Spirit. The unrenewed (natural) mind is at war with God. The renewed mind is the mind that thinks in agreement with the Holy Spirit and the truth. Thorough transformation of our soul, and even our body, can only come through a renewed mind.

B.   This is the apostolic mindset and lifestyle: agreement and fellowship with the Spirit. Paul placed much emphasis on the renewed mind. There is a quality of life in the Spirit that is available to those with a renewed mind that brings transformation to every aspect of life, and ultimately to our circumstances, our families, our cities, and nations. Faith is cultivated in the atmosphere of a renewed mind.

Those who live according to the flesh <u>set their minds</u> on the things of the flesh, but those who live according to the Spirit, the things of the Spirit. (Romans 8:5)

<u>Set your mind on things above</u>, not on things on the earth. For you died, and your life is hidden with Christ in God. (Colossians 3:2-3)

C.   The renewed mind only happens in the context of encounter. It is a radical re-orientation of our entire inner life. Every supernatural encounter in the Word and the Spirit is meant to change the way that we think. It is not simply a nice memory, but a revelation over which we are given stewardship. We must invest in these encounters by meditation and a change in our thinking, which will result in more encounters. When you experience something new in God, that experience is a "teaser" of our full inheritance. We must steward these experiences to bring increase.

His lord said to him, "Well done, good and faithful servant; you were faithful over a few things, I will make you ruler over many things. Enter into the joy of your lord"….For to everyone who has, more will be given, and he will have abundance; but from him who does not have, even what he has will be taken away. (Matthew 25:22, 29)

D.   The foundation of the renewed mind is the knowledge of God and his personality. His attributes and character form the foundation of all that we are, and they are the source of a renewed mind.

E.   Henri Nouwen speaks of turning our thought life from a monologue to a God-centered dialog with the Holy Spirit. Brother Lawrence called this principle of setting the mind on the indwelling Spirit "practicing the presence of God." The renewed mind involves an actual consciousness of God. Our mind is set on that which has our affections. God wants our affections on heavenly things.

F.   There are dimensions of the will of God that require our agreement. The Body of Christ must be in agreement with the Head. We literally "approve" of the will of God and pray and live accordingly. Our agreement with the will of God in prayer releases the purposes of God on the earth. The Lord has orchestrated the kingdom of God such that it requires agreement with the image bearers.

...that you may prove what is that good and acceptable and perfect will of God. (Romans 12:2)

For all the promises of God find their Yes in him. That is why it is though him that we utter our Amen to God for his glory. (2 Corinthians 1:20)

"Your kingdom come, your will be done, on earth as it is in heaven." (Matthew 6:10)

G.   We often do not know how much our thinking is being shaped (conformed) by the world and the flesh. There is great warfare over the mind of the believer. Example: Mark 6 (feeding of 5000). There is great temptation to define the "will of God" by our circumstances, past negative experiences, or emotions.

III.   THE POWER OF CONFESSION

Death and life are in the power of the tongue...(Proverbs 18:21)

Rejoice always, pray without ceasing, in everything give thanks; for this is the will of God in Christ Jesus for you. (1 Thessalonians 5:16-18)

The word is near you, in your mouth and in your heart...that is, the word of faith which we preach... with the mouth confession is made unto salvation [victory]. (Romans 10:8-10)

A.   It is possible to live with a renewed mind. All the Lord asks of us is to begin on this journey in a focused way. One of our greatest tools in this journey into thinking in agreement with the Spirit is confessing (literally speaking) to God the truths related to our identity and the knowledge of God.

B.   Many have thought that our confession unto salvation is a one-time event at our re-birth. A more full understanding of Romans 10 reveals that we are still being saved (in our soul and body) even now through confession of faith.

C.   Read it, write it, sing it, say it, and pray it. All the saints of old practiced "day and night" meditation on the word of God. This is the fastest way to a renewed mind.

> *...but his delight is in the law of the Lord, and on <u>his law he meditates day and night.</u> He is like a tree planted by streams of water that yields fruit in due season, and its leaf does not wither. In all that he does, he prospers. (Psalm 1:2-3)*

IV.   WALKING IN THE SPIRIT

> *I say then: walk in the Spirit, and you shall not fulfill the lust of the flesh. For the flesh lusts against the Spirit, and the Spirit against the flesh; and these are contrary to one another, so that you do not do the things that you wish. But if you are led by the Spirit, you are not under the law. (Galatians 5:16-18)*

A.   Paul explains that walking and fellowshipping with the indwelling Holy Spirit is actually the key to experiencing power over the lusts of the flesh. We are under a new law, the law of the Spirit. So, we are no longer instructed to attempt to accomplish righteousness by our own abilities (the flesh), but by the power of the Spirit who lives within us.

> *For the law of the Spirit of life in Christ Jesus has made me free from the law of sin and death. (Romans 8:2)*

B.   For many years, the phrase "walk in the Spirit" was a mystical, distant concept for me that I could not understand how to practically experience. I have since come to understand that this concept is extremely practical. To walk in the Spirit is simply to walk in unbroken fellowship with the Holy Spirit within us. In our fellowship with Him, we find superior pleasures and supernatural power, which is greater than the enticements of lust. I have found five simple expressions that are central to walking in the Spirit.

C. The first dimension of walking by the Spirit is simply ***talking to the Spirit.*** It is to maintain unbroken dialog with Christ in us. I actually have a prayer list, which I incorporate into my conversation with the Spirit, but the significant key is sincere conversation, which brings an orientation of our thinking into greater agreement with God.

D. The second expression of walking in the Spirit is ***meditation and confessing the word*** back to God, as mentioned above.

E. The third is ***praying in the Spirit*** continually.

F. The fourth is fellowshipping with the Spirit through ***silence and contemplative prayer.*** Some call this "soaking." I will explain this in detail below.

G. The fifth expression of walking in the Spirit is ***total obedience.*** This is what Paul referred to as being ***led by the Spirit.*** Total surrender to the will of God in all things is the only way to experience the fullness of God. Prayer is not enough. The difference between 100 percent obedience and 99 percent obedience is manifold. This does not mean that we have to succeed at every instant in obedience, but it does mean that we are living from a basic posture of radical obedience, and when we stumble, we stand up, repent, God hits delete, and we renew our commitment to total surrender and obedience.

V. FELLOWSHIPPING WITH THE SPIRIT

A. One of the greatest expressions of walking in the Spirit is fellowshipping with the Spirit directly as we sit and wait before him in silence. I encourage everyone to incorporate this practice into their daily life with God.

Have you not known? Have you not heard? The Lord is the everlasting God, the Creator of the ends of the earth. He does not faint or grow weary; his understanding is unsearchable. He gives power to the faint, and to him who has not might he increases strength. Even youths shall faint and grow weary, and young men shall fall exhausted; but they that wait upon the Lord shall renew their strength; they shall mount up with wings like eagles; they shall run and not be weary; they shall walk and not faint. (Isaiah 40:28-31)

For God alone my soul waits in silence, for my hope is from him. (Psalm 62:1)

B.   In this posture, we focus on our attention (mind) on the Spirit who lives inside us. Many times, we feel his presence in our "belly" area.

C.   It is often wise to begin a time of soaking or contemplative prayer with meditation on the scriptures, as mentioned above.

D.   As we fellowship with the Spirit, we begin to be silent before him. Keep your words few and simple. Just speak short phrases to him (ex. "Your love is better than wine; kiss me with your Word" or "Wash over my soul, Holy Spirit") followed by intervals of silence, all the while keeping your attention focused on his presence in you. I also encourage short periods of praying in tongues in this context.

E.   Your mind will begin to wander; it is helpful to redirect your mind with the word by praying the verse on which you have been meditating, then return to silence.

F.   You can also "visualize" a scripture or, specifically, the throne room (Rev.4-5) to keep your mind focused. The Lord may begin to give you internal visions and supernatural encounters at times while you wait before him. There are times when the Lord will even grant "trances" and out of body encounters with him.

G.   This tradition of contemplative prayer is thousands of years old. Many great men and women in the Spirit have gone deep in encounter with the Lord and fellowship with the Spirit by simply waiting before him for long hours. John called this posture being "in the Spirit" which is when he received the book of Revelation.

I was <u>in the Spirit</u> on the Lord's Day, and I heard behind me a loud voice…(Revelation 1:10)

H.   The experiences of those that have preceded us provoke us to go forward in into deeper communion with God through the Spirit. There is so much more available to us then we realize.

I.   Theresa of Avila wrote a famous work on prayer that has a unique emphasis on these "chamber encounters" with the Lord. She describes seven stages (or "mansions" as she calls them) of growth in this kind of intimate prayer. Her seven stages are only helpful in that they give us some of the process by which the Lord draws and carries us into deeper prayer. Some of the principles she highlights are as follows:

1.   Total surrender. There must be an intentionality to remove yourself from and rid yourself of the cares of this life. This is the beginning point of intimate prayer. Theresa constantly emphasized that this is not about learning a technique, but a love relationship with the Lord.

2.   Often after total surrender, we are torn between our abandonment to God and our previous preoccupation with the things of the world. There is sometimes great conflict of soul in this stage. We must learn to detach our heart from *all things* that are not from God. Many believers never make it beyond this stage.

3.   Soon, God will begin to give us an introduction to the experience of victory over sin in the grace of God and the tastes of deep joy that will happen later on as we grow in chamber encounters. This is to draw us and provoke us to love.

4.   Theresa speaks of "infused contemplation" which is "a divinely given...loving awareness of God"[13] and the presence of the Spirit within. Sometimes this is very subtle. Other times, it can be overwhelming. Brother Lawrence referred to this consciousness of God as "practicing the presence of God." Theresa actually speaks of periods of time in which the Lord "suspends the intellect." In other words, your mind actually quiets down for a period of time in an awareness of the presence of the Lord.

"At the moment that this prayer is given, the soul is captive...and is not free to love anything but God."[14]

---

[13] Dubay, Thomas. "Fire Within." p. 86.

[14] *Ibid.* p. 88

5. Teresa speaks of yet a deeper place of intimate prayer. At this point, the soul is almost completely absorbed in God. Sometimes for 15-20 minutes at a time, you literally lose awareness of anything else but God. A person is utterly transformed from one degree of glory to another in this intimate place of prayer.

> *"glorious foolishness....delight....incomparably greater than the previous prayer....a heavenly madness. Often I had been as though bewildered and inebriated in this love. The soul would desire to cry out praises....it cannot bear so much joy.....it would want to be all tongues to praise the Lord."[15]*

6. Teresa's sixth mansion (or stage) in prayer is where one begins to experience more dramatic chamber experiences with the Lord. This realm is still available today. She describes ecstasies (lasting sometimes for hours) where one is "fully awake" and "totally absorbed" in the things of God. She refers to "raptures, ecstasies, transports" (heavenly encounters), even levitation. In this kind of encounter, the Lord consumes the intellect and will, and sometimes one seems to be drunk with the love and presence of God. Sometimes these chamber encounters can last for days. Mystics of old called this "sober inebriation."

7. The seventh mansion for Teresa is a place of abiding and complete union with Christ. This is not just an occasional experience, but an ongoing manifestation of the presence of the Spirit within us. Sometimes this stage is less outwardly dramatic.

J. I encourage people to actively seek these deep encounters, but also to be patient in the process. Most often, more dramatic encounters with the Lord come suddenly, but require a lifestyle of pursuit, which will inevitably result in heavenly encounters through the Holy Spirit. Have patience and do not give up. This is a significant part of our priestly ministry.

---

[15] *Ibid.* p. 94.

K. Do not despise the smaller encounters. The small movements of the heart have eternal impact.

L. It is important to note that God does not live in any man-made system. It is not entirely uncommon for God to release what Theresa speaks of as "sixth mansion" encounters in believers that have been walking with the Lord for only a very short period of time. These encounters with the indwelling Spirit are not a matter of our works or righteousness, but come freely through the finished work of Christ! Theresa's stages only indicate that there is a process of surrender and agreement required on our part, which usually comes in progressive stages. We learn from Theresa that there is more available then we are currently experiencing, and that we should not lose heart as we press on towards the upward call of God in Christ.

Session 7: The Heavenly Symphony – Throne Room Life

I.   OUR HEAVENLY CALLING

A.   It is essential that we understand our full identification with Christ in his priestly ministry. He is one with us in our humanity and sin on the cross, and we are one with his resurrection and ascension. He became as we were in order to enable us to become as he is. We are one spirit with him. Therefore, we are seated with Christ on the heavenly throne.

> *But he who is joined to the Lord is one spirit with Him. (1 Corinthians 6:17)*

> *…and raised us up together, and made us sit together in the heavenly places in Christ Jesus (Ephesians 2:6)*

B.   Our calling as priests is essentially heavenly. We live in heavenly places right now through our union with Christ. That is where our life is hidden with Christ in God. Jesus' ascension was our ascension. Our truest life is with Jesus right now.

> *Therefore, holy brethren, <u>partakers of the heavenly calling</u>, consider the Apostle and High Priest of our confession, Christ Jesus (Hebrews 3:1)*

> *For you died, and your life is hidden with Christ in God. (Colossians 3:3)*

C.   Christ's seat in heaven speaks of his authority over all powers and principalities and also his intimacy with the Father. Both of these are ours in Christ's (and our) enthronement.

> *…that you may know what is the hope of His calling, what are the riches of the glory of His inheritance in the saints, and what is the exceeding greatness of His power toward us who believe, according to the working of His mighty power which He worked in Christ when He raised Him from the dead and seated Him at His right hand in the heavenly places, far above all principality and power and might and dominion, and every name that is named, not only in this age but also in that which is to come. And He put all things under His feet, and gave Him to be head over all things to the church, which is His body, the fullness of Him who fills all in all. (Ephesians 1:18-23)*

D. There are two sides to this truth of our ascension with Christ. It has been called the "legal" side and the "vital" side. The legal side is the reality that we already have this position in heaven of intimacy and authority with Christ. The vital side is the outworking of this in our experience in our soul and body, which is progressive. In other words, we have it all in our spirit, but we are growing in the experience of the finished work of Christ in our soul and body. We will experience the fullness when we are given new bodies at the resurrection and experience the fullness of our heavenly calling in the New Jerusalem.

For in this we groan, earnestly desiring to be clothed with our habitation which is from heaven (2 Corinthians 5:2)

II.   A NEW AND LIVING WAY: THRONE LIFE

A. Hebrews 10:19-23 is the thesis verse of the entire book of Hebrews. Jesus opened up a new and living way into the very presence of the Father. In the Old Covenant, only one man, one time per year could enter into the manifest glory of God. Now, Jesus has made a way, a new way, which is through his own work of atonement.

Therefore, brethren, having boldness to enter the Holiest by the blood of Jesus, by a new and living way which He consecrated for us, through the veil, that is, His flesh, and having a High Priest over the house of God, let us draw near with a true heart in full assurance of faith, having our hearts sprinkled from an evil conscience and our bodies washed with pure water. Let us hold fast the confession of our hope without wavering, for He who promised is faithful. (Hebrews 10:19-23)

Seeing then that we have a great High Priest who has passed through the heavens, Jesus the Son of God, let us hold fast our confession. For we do not have a High Priest who cannot sympathize with our weaknesses, but was in all points tempted as we are, yet without sin. Let us therefore come boldly to the throne of grace, that we may obtain mercy and find grace to help in time of need. (Hebrews 4:14-16)

B. To enter to the holy place is to enter into the heavenly sanctuary. We are called to interact with the heavenly throne room and the One seated on the throne through the finished work of Jesus.

> *For Christ has not entered the holy places made with hands, which are copies of the true, but <u>into heaven itself, now to appear in the presence of God for us</u> (Hebrews 9:24)*

C. After being with Jesus for months and observing his relationship with the Father and the power of the Spirit flowing through him, the disciples had one very essential request: Teach us to pray! They recognized that Jesus' life and ministry was heavenly. His teaching and miracles were from another realm. They knew that prayer was the secret to his life. Jesus leaned on the Father and Spirit in prayer, and he lived from heaven to earth.

> *Now it came to pass, as He was praying in a certain place, when He ceased, that one of His disciples said to Him, "Lord, teach us to pray, as John also taught his disciples." (Luke 11:1)*

> *No one has ascended to heaven but He who came down from heaven, that is, the Son of Man <u>who is in heaven</u>. (John 3:13)*

D. When Jesus was teaching the disciples to pray, he taught them to start in heaven. In prayer, Jesus instructs us to focus our mind on the Father and the heavenly throne room.

> *Our <u>Father in heaven</u>, hallowed be Your name. Your kingdom come. Your will be done on earth as it is in heaven. (Matthew 6:9-10)*

E. The Apostle Paul taught this same principle. We are to set our minds on the third heaven. Heaven is a literal city that will come down to earth (Rev 21). There is a real throne room where the Father and Christ are seated right now. Focusing our attention and meditation on the throne as revealed in Revelation 4-5 is central to our growth in prayer.

> *If then you were raised with Christ, seek those things which are above, where Christ is, sitting at the right hand of God. Set your mind on things above, not on things on the earth. For you died, and your life is hidden with Christ in God. When Christ who is our life appears, then you also will appear with Him in glory. (Colossians 3:1-4)*

Therefore we do not lose heart. Even though our outward man is perishing, yet the inward man is being renewed day by day. For our light affliction, which is but for a moment, is working for us a far more exceeding and eternal weight of glory, while we do not look at the things which are seen, but at the things which are not seen. For the things which are seen are temporary, but the things which are not seen are eternal. (2 Corinthians 4:16-18)

F. Heaven is a literal place on which we focus our mediation, but it is also a quality of life or a mode of being. Heaven is where the presence of God is being manifest. Our calling is to gaze, meditate, and experience the literal throne room, even while we are experiencing and contending for the atmosphere and reality of heaven to manifest on the earth. We are ambassadors of the eternal city in this age.

G. There are four significant dimensions to our interaction with the heavenly throne room right now:

1. *By faith* we appropriate the fact that we are already seated there with Christ. We live in a place of intimacy and dominion right now by faith. We live a heavenly life by faith.

2. We literally *draw near* to the throne (Hebrews 4:16; Colossians 3:1-4). This means we "approach" the throne in prayer. Every time we pray and worship, we are interacting with the One that is seated on the throne. It is not a vain imagination to think of ourselves as standing on the sea of glass before the throne speaking directly to the Father in prayer. This is our reality in prayer.

3. In the place of prayer, we *gaze* and *encounter* the one seated on the throne as we *meditate* on the realities around the throne room.

4. In the body or out, your spirit *actually enters* heaven. These are actual, heavenly, out of body experiences, which occur in a trance or dream. These encounters will happen to many as we near the return of Jesus. On a lesser level, one can have internal visions from the Holy Spirit as we approach the throne of God in prayer and meditation. But there are times when, in a trance, the Lord takes someone's spirit out of their body to heaven. This is the context of Revelation 4-5, Isaiah 6, and Ezekiel 1.

It is doubtless not profitable for me to boast. I will come to visions and revelations of the Lord: I know a man in Christ who fourteen years ago— whether in the body I do not know, or whether out of the body I do not know, God knows—such a one was caught up to the third heaven. And I know such a man—whether in the body or out of the body I do not know, God knows— how he was caught up into Paradise and heard inexpressible words, which it is not lawful for a man to utter. (2 Corinthians 12:1-4)

III.   THE HEAVENLY SYMPHONY

A.   The entire created order is "throne centered," meaning everything that transpires must "get approval" from the One seated on the throne. The knowledge of this heavenly court is at the very core of our journey into the knowledge and splendor of God.

B.   Understanding and encountering the throne room and the One seated on the throne is the doorway into the library of the attributes and person of God. This is the great "Mt. Everest" of the Kingdom of God. As we gaze on the throne, our lives will increasingly be oriented around these eternal realities.

C.   We refer to the throne room – as revealed in Revelation 4-5, Daniel 7, Ezekiel 1, and Isaiah 6 – as the *heavenly symphony*. The throne room is the highest revelation of the splendor of God. Every feature, sound, and color displays the unparalleled beauty of God. We will spend eternity unpacking the revelation of the holy in this place. This is the ultimate fulfillment of Psalm 27:4.

One thing I have asked from the LORD, that I shall seek: That I may dwell in the house of the LORD all the days of my life, to <u>behold</u> the <u>beauty of the LORD</u> and to <u>meditate</u> in His temple. (Psalm 27:4)

I will meditate on the glorious splendor of Your majesty, and on Your wondrous works. (Psalm 145:5)

D.   **Revelation 4-5** is the most detailed and highest revelation of the throne of God in scripture.

E.	There are undoubtedly tens of thousands of activities, sounds, colors, fragrances, and dynamics around the throne. The Holy Spirit specifically chose to reveal about 30-40 features of the heavenly symphony to us in scripture. Every one of these features of the throne and the One seated on the throne is a window into an endless flow of revelation into the being of the uncreated God.

F.	Humanly speaking, God began with a blank slate. We must ask the question of why every feature of the throne room even exists. What is the Lord revealing of his glory through each feature he chooses to reveal? The Holy Spirit is strategic in what he has revealed of the throne to us. It is designed to produce the first and greatest commandment in us.

G.	Our journey into the heavenly symphony and throne room realities is like learning a new culture or language. It takes time. It is normal for our heart to not respond at first, but given time, prayer, and meditation, our heart will connect to the beauty and fascination of God.

H.	In prayer, we are not speaking to the air. We are speaking to the One on the throne. The revelation of the throne gives relevance to our life and prayers.

## IV.	GOING THROUGH THE OPEN DOOR (REVELATION 4)

A.	***Behold, a door standing open in heaven!*** – The first thing that John encounters in Revelation 4 is an open door. This was a real door through which John travelled in the Spirit, but in a general way, Jesus has opened a door to every believer to access heavenly realities.

I am the door. If anyone enters by Me, he will be saved… (John 10:9)

B.	***At once I was in the Spirit*** – We encounter God through the person of the Holy Spirit. As we walk in agreement with the Spirit as a lifestyle, encounter will increase. Many times, developing a long history of fellowship and agreement with the Spirit will lead to new dimensions of heavenly encounter.

C.	***A throne stood in heaven*** – The throne speaks of the unchallenged sovereignty of God. According to Daniel 7 and Ezekiel 1, the throne is sapphire in color and is mingled with fire. There is a river of fire proceeding from it. The throne is filled with light and color, engulfed in fire. God actually clothes himself in light, which includes all the colors in the spectrum.

Who covers Yourself with light as with a garment… (Psalm 104:2)

who alone has immortality, <u>dwelling in unapproachable light</u>, whom no man has seen or can see, to whom be honor and everlasting power. Amen. (1 Timothy 6:16)

D. *One seated on the throne* – When we pray, we are not speaking to the air. We are speaking to the person of God, who is our Father, and is pleased with us. Within the very being of God and all his attributes, is the greatest pleasure that can ever be experienced. For us, in Christ, it is a throne of *grace*.

 Let us therefore come boldly to the throne of grace, that we may obtain mercy and find grace to help in time of need. (Hebrews 4:16)

E. *And he who sat there had the appearance of jasper and sardius* – Jasper is a translucent green stone (though it comes in multiple colors with green being the predominant). Sardius is a deep red stone.

 The jasper speaks of the mystery and beauty of his person. He is filled with splendor beyond what our imagination can conceive of. In fact, C.S. Lewis wrote that he believed that God gave us our imagination for the primary purpose of mediation on heaven!

 The red speaks of God's deep passion and desire. The desire of God is one of the greatest themes of his character. He has all-power and deep, passionate desire. *This means that his desire (purpose) comes to pass.*

F. *Around the throne was a rainbow that had the appearance of an emerald* – Ezekiel also saw this rainbow. Clearly, this rainbow is the predecessor of the rainbows on the earth. God gave us the meaning of the rainbow! It speaks of his covenant of mercy and kindness towards humans. It speaks of his kind disposition towards us! The One on the throne is full of loving-kindness and compassion!

I have set my rainbow in the clouds, and it will be the sign of the covenant between me and the earth. Whenever I bring clouds over the earth and the rainbow appears in the clouds, I will remember my covenant between me and you and all living creatures of every kind. Never again will the waters become a flood to destroy all life. Whenever the rainbow appears in the clouds, I will see it and remember the everlasting covenant between God and all living creatures of every kind on the earth. (Genesis 9:13-16)

G.   *Around the throne were twenty-four thrones…on the thrones were twenty-four elders* – I believe these twenty-four elders are robed, enthroned, and crowned humans. Once again, the inconceivable dignity of the human race is manifest. We are forever the highest expression of the government of the eternal city.

To him who overcomes I will grant to sit with Me on My throne, as I also overcame and sat down with My Father on His throne. (Rev. 3:21)

H.   *From the throne came flashes of lightening, and rumblings (literal sounds), and peals of thunders* – From the very being of God there is sound that has creative power. He is speaking from his holy hill. This same phenomenon is mentioned elsewhere in the book of Revelation as taking place on the earth in the context of God's judgments (Rev. 8:2; 11:19).

I.   *And before the throne were seven torches of fire, which are the seven spirits of God* – This is the manifestation of the Holy Spirit around the throne in his fullness. Incidentally, he is also fully dwelling in our spirit.

The Spirit of the LORD will rest on him— the Spirit of wisdom and of understanding, the Spirit of counsel and of might, the Spirit of the knowledge and fear of the LORD. (Isaiah 11:2)

J.   *And before the throne there as it were a sea of glass, like crystal* – This is the great gathering place before the throne. It also speaks of God's transcendence. It is sapphire in color. This sea predated the oceans of the earth. It speaks of God's great majesty.

Then Moses went up, also Aaron, Nadab, and Abihu, and seventy of the elders of Israel, and they saw the God of Israel. And there was under His feet as it were a paved work of sapphire stone, and it was like the very heavens in its clarity. But on the nobles of the children of Israel He did not lay His hand. So they saw God, and they ate and drank. (Numbers 24:9-11)

The likeness of the firmament above the heads of the living creatures was like the color of an awesome crystal, stretched out over their heads. (Ezekiel 1:22)

K. *And around the throne…are four living creatures* – These creatures preceded the earthly creatures which they resemble. They are seraphim. They are one of two angelic orders closest to the throne. The cherubim are beneath the sea of glass while these four seraphim are flying around the throne. Their function is both unending, unrelenting adoration, which flows from revelation of God, and also governmental responsibilities. Because they are covered with eyes, they are designed to behold the Lord and are therefore a manifestation of what God is like, each in their own unique way.

And they do not rest day or night, saying: "Holy, holy, holy, Lord God Almighty, Who was and is and is to come!" (Revelation 4:8)

V. CONCLUSION

A. Our priestly ministry of day and night prayer and worship only makes sense in light of a throne centered reality. God could have put whatever he wanted around the throne room. Every detail is significant to our hearts growing in love and confidence.

B. Ultimately, this throne room exists as a platform for God to relate to the created order. His is not limited to this throne room in any way.

But who is able to build Him a temple, since heaven and the heaven of heavens cannot contain Him? (2 Chronicles 2:6)

Session 8: Singing Prophets and Priests – Heavenly Worship

I.   **REVIEW: DAVID'S VOW**

    A. David's throne is the throne that Jesus will sit upon. Therefore, it was imperative that David exemplify the core values of the Kingdom of the Messiah.

    B. Central to David's value system was his passion for God's <u>manifest glory</u> to dwell with Israel in Jerusalem. He was consumed with this vision that was God's original purpose in the creation of man – to find a dwelling place. This was David's first priority as king.

    C. David made a vow to not live a "business as usual" life until God had a dwelling place on earth. David knew that God wanted to manifest himself through his people.

    D. David is a picture of what God is releasing on the church at the end of the age. History began with a resting place of God with men (Gen. 1-2), and it ends with a full manifestation of God's dwelling with men (Rev. 20-22).

    E. David took an actual vow. He would not pursue his personal comfort or build his own kingdom until God's dwelling was established (Ps. 132).

    F. Towards this end, David quickly instituted priestly ministry upon his arrival as king of Israel in Jerusalem. Central to this priestly ministry was 4,288 full-time singers and musicians. This is known as David's Tabernacle.

    G. God promises to rebuild David's Tabernacle.

> *After this I will return and will rebuild the tabernacle of David, which has fallen down; I will rebuild its ruins and I will set it up (Acts 15:16)*

    H. As a new covenant priesthood, prophetic singing and musicianship is at the top of God's strategy to release the greatest revival that the world has yet seen as well as the coming judgments.

II.   PROPHETIC WORSHIP AND THE COMING CREATIVE RENNAISANCE

A. Prophetic music is not the "warm up" for preaching. Music and creativity have a strategic role in the coming eschatological revival and judgments. Prophetic music literally releases the Kingdom of God and shifts the atmosphere over regions.

B. By the term "prophetic worship," we are simply referring to music and creative expression that comes from the Holy Spirit moving on our spirit. This can simply be our spontaneous response to God's touch on our heart, but it can also refer to the voice of the Lord through song, dance, visual arts, sound, etc.

C. David trained and modeled prophetic worship in his tabernacle.

> *Moreover David and the captains of the army separated for the service some of the sons of Asaph, of Heman, and of Jeduthun, who <u>should prophesy with harps, stringed instruments, and cymbals</u>. And the number of the skilled men performing their service was: Of the sons of Asaph: Zaccur, Joseph, Nethaniah, and Asharelah; the sons of Asaph were under the direction of Asaph, <u>who prophesied according to the order of the king.</u> Of Jeduthun, the sons of Jeduthun: Gedaliah, Zeri, Jeshaiah, Shimei, Hashabiah, and Mattithiah, six, under the direction of their father Jeduthun, who <u>prophesied with a harp</u> to give thanks and to praise the LORD. (1 Chronicles 25:1-3)*

D. The Lord dwells in our praise. He releases his life in the context of praise (Ps. 22:3). David understood this principle. Praise brings us into agreement with the adoration of the uncreated God and with one another in the Spirit. Through this union, power is released and God is tangibly present.

E. Music, prayer, and prophecy are interconnected in the Spirit. The worship movement is the prophetic movement. The prophetic movement is the prayer movement.

> *"But now bring me a musician." Then it happened, when the musician played, that the hand of the LORD came upon him. And he said, "Thus says the LORD…" (2 Kings 3:15)*

F. Isaiah speaks of a new (prophetic) song that will cover the earth in the generation in which the Lord will return. There is a song and a sound of praise that the world has not yet heard; it will be motivated by deep love in the end time church. It is new, in terms of being a present-tense overflow of the heart of millions of people to the Lord, and it will cover the earth.

> *<u>They shall lift up their voice, they shall sing</u> (the nations); for the majesty of the LORD. They shall cry aloud from the sea. Therefore glorify the LORD in the dawning light, the name of the LORD God of Israel in the coastlands of the sea. From the ends of the earth we have heard songs: 'Glory to the righteous!'...On that day the Lord will punish the host of heaven, in heaven, and the kings of the earth, on the earth. (Isaiah 24:14-16, 23)*

> *Sing to the LORD a <u>new song</u> and His praise from the ends of the earth, you who go down to the sea, and all that is in it, you coastlands and you inhabitants of them! Let the wilderness and its cities lift up their voice, the villages that Kedar inhabits. Let the inhabitants of Sela sing; let them shout from the top of the mountains. Let them give glory to the LORD and declare His praise in the coastlands. The LORD shall go forth like a mighty man; He shall stir up His zeal like a man of war. He shall cry out, yes, shout aloud; He shall prevail against His enemies. "I have held My peace a long time, I have been still and restrained Myself. Now I will cry like a woman in labor, I will pant and gasp at once." (Isaiah 42:10-14)*

G. This eschatological song will not just accompany the return of Jesus, but it will be a significant part of releasing the great shakings, revival, and the second coming. Our song has governmental authority and function.

H. There is a literal song of deliverance that the eschatological church will express. Paul and Silas got a foretaste of this in Acts 16.

> *You will protect me from trouble and surround me with <u>songs of deliverance</u>. (Psalm 32:7)*

> *But at midnight Paul and Silas were praying and singing hymns to God, and the prisoners were listening to them. Suddenly there was a great earthquake, so that the foundations of the prison were shaken; and immediately all the doors were opened and everyone's chains were loosed. And the keeper of the prison, awaking from sleep and seeing the prison doors open, supposing the prisoners had fled, drew his sword and was about to kill himself. But Paul called with a loud voice, saying, "Do yourself no harm, for we are all here." Then he called for a light, ran in, and fell down trembling before Paul and Silas. And he brought them out and said, "Sirs, what must I do to be saved?" (Acts 16:25-29)*

I. In the genius and romance of God, he has designed government in the Kingdom to function in conjunction with singers, musicians, and creativity. Heaven, the governmental center of the universe, is filled with sounds, singing, music, and prayer. It is in this way that the Lord releases his government.

Now when He had taken the scroll, the four living creatures and the twenty-four elders fell down before the Lamb, <u>each having a harp, and golden bowls full of incense</u>, which are the prayers of the saints. (Revelation 5:8)

And from the throne proceeded lightnings, thunderings, and voices [sounds]. (Revelation 4:5)

For My house shall be called a house of prayer for all nations. (Isaiah 56:7)

   a. The Hebrew word for "prayer" in Isaiah 56:7 is actually a word that means "hymn" or a sung prayer. This is the Jewish custom, to this day, in prayer.

J. The highest purpose of song is to express divine transcendence. This is the song that surrounds the throne. When we pray on earth as it is in heaven, it involves this very heavenly worship being poured out on the earth.

The four living creatures, each having six wings, were full of eyes around and within. And they do not rest day or night, saying: Holy, Holy, Holy is the Lord God Almighty, who was, and is, and is to come. (Revelation 4:8)

III. SOUND, LIGHT, AND THE SPIRIT OF PROPHECY

A. The day that God created light is the day that music and sound began. Light and sound travel through the medium of waves. Moving light waves are called electromagnetic waves. Humans are only able to see about 3 percent of the light spectrum. Part of the 97 percent that we cannot see is categorized as electromagnetic light. Within electromagnetic light there is a range of waves known as radio waves. A small portion of the spectrum of radio waves is audible sound, which the human ear can perceive. So, light and sound are on the same spectrum. This was the first thing that God created and is the foundation of everything else in creation. God's voice has creative power.

> *Let there be light…(Genesis 1:3)*

B.   God created light and sound (music) before there was a sun. This light was a revelation of his own glory and person.

> *God is light…(1 John 1:4)*

C.   Human beings have been given the unique creative ability to release the sound of God through music, speech, singing, sounds, and creativity. The sound of God always releases substance. He creates and changes. We can shift nations by the creativity of God.

D.   Indeed, if God is, in his very essence, the Creator, how much more should the prophetic church move in unsurpassed creativity in every realm of culture as an expression of the government of God?

IV.   MUSIC HISTORY AND THE CHURCH

A.   As a music major in a secular college, I studied the tabernacle of David and early Jewish music because it was the most advanced of its time. David was a musician. This was designed by God to be a central part of the Messianic Kingdom. David actually played music to the Lord seven times per day (Ps 119:164)! This practice enabled David to not only influence his generation politically, but also prophetically, poetically, and culturally. He led their spiritual and cultural life through the song of the Lord.

B.   As I studied music history, I was fascinated to discover that most of the significant musical advances in history were through believers. Our first few semesters were dedicated almost exclusively to church music.

C.   A very significant shift happened in the church during the protestant reformation. Luther and the reformers observed that the music of the church was not being written for congregational singing as much as for highly skilled musicians.

D. So, Luther took bar tunes of his day and wrote hymns to their tune with the emphasis being on making them sing-able.

E. Something significant was gained through this, but something was also lost. The positive was that hymns were reintroduced ("the folk songs of the church"). The negative was that the more highly skilled musicians no longer had a place in corporate gatherings of the church to release the heights of their creativity. I believe that the Lord wants to restore both of these dimensions in the coming creative renaissance. The highest dimensions of creative expression should find a place in the house of prayer. And there will be supernatural authority through the voice of the Lord.

V. PAULINE THEOLOGY AND SINGING

A. Paul instructed the early church in singing. He had an understanding of the role of singing. This is an often-overlooked aspect of Pauline theology. This is not an after-thought for Paul. It was a key to the success of the church.

And do not be drunk with wine, in which is dissipation; but be filled with the Spirit, speaking to one another in psalms and hymns and spiritual songs, singing and making melody in your heart to the Lord, giving thanks always for all things to God the Father in the name of our Lord Jesus Christ, submitting to one another in the fear of God. (Ephesians 5:18-21)

Let the word of Christ dwell in you richly in all wisdom, teaching and admonishing one another in psalms and hymns and spiritual songs, singing with grace in your hearts to the Lord. (Colossians 3:16)

B. For two thousand years, the church has been singing almost every time we gather, but most people never stop to think about the purpose of this singing. This is largely because of Paul's teaching. But Paul had clear understanding in his instruction to the early church on singing.

C. Paul connected singing with two vital realities: being filled with the Spirit and the Word dwelling richly within us. This is a corporate reality. We will feel God more and know his Word and Person more as we sing. Our experience of God increases as we *sing*, not as we simply read or study primarily (though these have high value as well).

D.   There are three expressions of song that Paul highlights, all of which are vital to understand.

1.   Psalms – This refers to the practice of singing from the Bible. We practice this in our "Worship with the Word" sets. Paul knew that when we sing the Bible, it transcends our intellect and touches every part of our person including our emotions and our spirit. So, the word begins to dwell richly as we encounter Jesus in the Word.

2.   Hymns – Hymns are pre-written songs that often contain doctrine and emphasize the knowledge of God or expressions of praise and intimacy. I classify all of our worship songs in the category of hymns.

3.   Spiritual Songs – This is perhaps the most overlooked dimension of singing in the church. The Greek word Paul uses here is "odais pneumatikais," which means "Spirit song." This refers to spontaneous singing and corporate singing in the Spirit. This was a normal part of church life in the apostolic church.

E.   Singing in the Spirit was an important part of Paul's personal life and the expression of the apostolic church.

What is the conclusion then? I will pray with the spirit, and I will also pray with the understanding. I will sing with the spirit, and I will also sing with the understanding. (1 Corinthians 14:15)

I thank God that I speak with tongues more than you all. (1 Corinthians 14:18)

VI.   BENEFITS OF SINGING IN THE SPIRIT: ENGAGING THE SPIRIT OF REVELATION

A.   Know the mysteries of the Kingdom (Matt. 13:11)

B.   Edify yourself (1 Cor. 14:4)

C.   Dislodge the powers of darkness (Eph 6)

D.   Utter mysteries (1 Cor. 14:2)

E.   Proclaim the wonderful works of God. (Acts 2:11)

F.   Release supernatural ministry (Acts 2) (Azusa example)

G.   Releases the Spirit of Revelation and Wisdom

VII. DAVID'S VOW WILL BE EXPRESSED IN THE END-TIME WORSHIP MOVEMENT: FULL-TIME MUSICIANS

A.   The Holy Spirit's End-Time worship and prayer movement (Rev. 22:17; 5:8; 8:4; Lk. 18:7-8; Mt.25:1-13; Isa. 62:6- 7; 24:14-16; 25:9; 26:8-9; 27:2-5, 13; 30:18-19; 42:10-13; 43:26;51:11; 52:8; Joel 2:12-17, 32; Jer. 31:7; Mic. 5:3-4; Zeph. 2:1-3; Ps. 102:17-20; 122:6; Zech. 12:10, etc.).

I saw thrones, and they [saints] sat on them…They lived and reigned with Christ for 1000 years…They shall reign with Him 1000 years. (Revelation 20:4-6)

B.   The kings of the earth will be saved, worship Jesus (Ps. 72:11; 102:15; 138:4; 148:11; Isa. 62:2; Rev. 21:24), and base their national governments on God's Word.

All kings shall fall down before Him; all nations shall serve Him. (Psalm 72:11)

C.   The End-Time worship movement will call Jesus to the earth at the time of the

Second Coming. The Millennial worship movement will call the Father to the earth (Rev. 21:3). It is central to the Lord's strategy to raise up full-time musicians, singers, and artisans to cover the earth with his glory.

The Spirit and the Bride say, "Come!" (Rev. 22:17)

D. It is critical to understand that this movement of worship, intercession, and revival will not come to fullness without full-time musicians and singers. What David did under the old covenant was but a shadow of the greater reality under the new covenant. The concept of full-time singers and musicians in the house of prayer is new to many, but is actually intensely practical when you understand what happens with prophetic singing and musicianship.

E. The Book of Revelation speaks of a movement of worship and intercession in Jerusalem at the end of the age.

> *Then I looked, and behold, a Lamb standing on Mount Zion, and with Him one hundred and forty-four thousand, having His Father's name written on their foreheads. And I heard a voice from heaven, like the voice of many waters, and like the voice of loud thunder. And I heard the sound of harpists playing their harps. They sang as it were a new song before the throne, before the four living creatures, and the elders; and no one could learn that song except the hundred and forty-four thousand who were redeemed from the earth. These are the ones who were not defiled with women, for they are virgins. These are the ones who follow the Lamb wherever He goes. These were redeemed from among men, being firstfruits to God and to the Lamb. And in their mouth was found no deceit, for they are without fault before the throne of God. (Revelation 14:1-5)*

F. *Sons of Thunder prophecy by James Ryle (See Addendum 1)*

Session 9: Priestly Mitigation – Understanding Joel's Two Trumpets

Hear this, you elders, and give ear, all you inhabitants of the land! Has anything like this happened in your days, or even in the days of your fathers? (Joel 1:2)

He answered and said to them, "When it is evening you say, 'It will be fair weather, for the sky is red'; and in the morning, 'It will be foul weather today, for the sky is red and threatening.' Hypocrites! You know how to discern the face of the sky, but you cannot discern the signs of the times." (Matthew 16:2-3)

I. DISCERNING THE TIMES: THE CALL TO HEAR

A. It is critical that we understand the times in which we live from God's perspective. In April of 2009, Allen Hood preached a message at Awaken the Dawn which was a prophetic confirmation of the urgency of the hour in which we live in America. That message, on Joel 1-2, was a turning point for our community in terms of our sobriety and the earnestness of our call to embrace the principles of Joel 1-2. America is at critical juncture at this time. I believe the next 5 years will determine the future destiny of our nation. History truly belongs to the intercessors. Over the last 2 years, our call to intercession became increasingly about our children and their destiny.

B. The message of Joel 2 is absolutely central to our calling in Fredericksburg. We must have understanding of the day of the Lord, which Joel speaks of and of our call to a radical response in intercession and repentance. Right before we launched the Prayer Furnace, I felt the Lord speak to me, "Joel 2 is your plan A and there is no plan B." We are called to operate in the spirit of Joel 2 as a community. This is one of the great banner passages over the end-time prayer movement.

C. Joel was prophesying to a nation in crisis. America is in crisis. There is an emerging prospect of a post-Christian America, which will identify more with the anti-christ system and ideology than with the Kingdom of God.

   1. Builders generation (born between 1924-1944) – 65% church engagement

   2. Boomers generation (born between 1945-1965) – 35% church engagement

   3. Buster generation (born between 1966-1983) – 15% church engagement

4.   Bridger generation (born after 1984) – 4% church engagement[16]

D. Critical missiological milestones:

1.   2% of population – the reality is most likely here to stay

2.   10% of population – the reality is probably capable of spontaneous reproduction.

3.   16% of population – threshold of catalytic reproduction/multiplication

E. We are in a Joel 1-2 moment in America at this time. Mike Bickle saw an angel in an open vision right after Hurricane Katrina who put a trumpet to his lips three times in a row indicating that we are about to experience crises that transcend Katrina in their scope. He also saw, in an open vision, tanks driving across our land. God sent Bill Bright a word which he published in 1995 in his book ***The Coming Revival*** calling the millions of leaders in the church of America to forty-day fasts to avert coming judgment on our nation and to ask the Lord for revival and mercy.

F. We have murdered over 53 million babies in their mother's womb over the last thirty years. We are now promoting homosexuality and every kind of perversion on a level that was unthought-of just a few decades ago. Many of the basic doctrines of the faith, such as the reality of hell and the deity of Christ, are under a full frontal assault within the church at this time. God cannot stand back and watch a nation that, at one time was mostly Christian, embrace this kind of iniquity and not act. Jesus is a righteous judge. And judgment begins with the house of God.

G. Joel's first statement is for us.

Hear this, you elders, and give ear, all you inhabitants of the land! Has anything like this happened in your days, or even in the days of your fathers? (Joel 1:2)

H. Joel calls Israel to hear. To hear is when our spiritual senses are fully awakened to the reality of the word of the Lord – when the word of the Lord touches us at the deepest level and moves beyond an abstract concept with which we have a familiarity. This *requires* an active engagement with what the Holy Spirit is saying and doing in this hour. It is a summons to a people, not just an individual.

---

[16] Rainer, Thomas. *The Bridger Generation*. Nashville, TN: Broadman & Holman Pub. 2006, p. 169.

I. Joel asks if they have seen anything like the judgment, which Israel had ***already*** experienced. I would ask the same question today; does anyone remember anything like what has transpired even in the last few years in terms of the onslaught of iniquity and the beginning of judgments? There is a rhetorical answer to this question. We are in a season unlike anything that anyone alive has ever experienced. Extreme times do require extreme measures.

J. The prophet Jeremiah cried out, "O my soul, my soul! I am pained in my very heart! My heart makes a noise in me; I cannot hold my peace, because you have heard, O my soul, the sound of the trumpet, the alarm of war." (Jer. 4:19)

K. Interestingly, today as I was writing this, I got an email from a prophetic friend of mine saying that he had dreamed last night that God was calling the Prayer Furnace to embrace the "sacred heart." Then he woke up to his toddler daughter asking him if he could hear "that sound." "What sound?" he asked. "My heart," she said, "can you hear yours?"

L. Jesus warned about receiving that which we hear from the Lord as being very important to him. This speaks of our response to what we are hearing.

Then He said to them, "Take heed what you hear. With the same measure you use, it will be measured to you; and to you who hear, more will be given. For whoever has, to him more will be given; but whoever does not have, even what he has will be taken away from him." (Mark 4:24-25)

Therefore take heed how you hear. For whoever has, to him more will be given; and whoever does not have, even what he seems to have will be taken from him. (Luke 18:18)

II. JOEL'S CRISIS

Hear this, you elders, and give ear, all you inhabitants of the land! Has anything like this happened in your days, or even in the days of your fathers? Tell your children about it, let your children tell their children, and their children another generation. What the chewing locust left, the swarming locust has eaten; what the swarming locust left, the crawling locust has eaten; and what the crawling locust left, the consuming locust has eaten. (Joel 1:2-4)

A. Joel is prophesying in the context of Israel having just experienced a great economic disaster in the form of a locust plague.

B. Joel is standing after the crisis of locusts in an agrarian society, and he prophesies that greater crisis is coming if they do not return to the Lord.

    a. Joel is standing between two great crises. He is in a window when there is potential for mercy instead of judgment based on a response of repentance and intercession.

    b. He is calling the nation to hear the reality of their situation and respond rightly. He gives the primary remedy in the midst of a crisis of this order: corporate prayer and fasting and repentance. He calls for a radical returning to the Lord and a cry of intercession. It is always tempting to think, according to the natural, that

the main remedy in crisis is to simply move into a self-preservation mode, but Joel calls us to mitigate as a royal priesthood! This is God's central remedy.

Gird yourselves and lament, you priests; wail, you who minister before the altar; come, lie all night in sackcloth, you who minister to my God; for the grain offering and the drink offering are withheld from the house of your God. Consecrate a fast, call a sacred assembly; gather the elders and all the inhabitants of the land into the house of the LORD your God, and cry out to the LORD. (Joel 1:13-14)

E. Joel calls for radical measures. And he gives his reason:

Alas for the day! For the day of the LORD is at hand; it shall come as destruction from the Almighty. (Joel 1:15)

F. Right now, in America, we are in a lull between two crises. We just experienced a close equivalent to Israel's locust plague in our recent financial recession, and apart from repentance, a greater crisis is coming. We must not be lulled to sleep in the midst of a delay between crises!

III. WHERE IS GOD IN THE MIDST OF CRISIS?

A. In order to understand God's role in the midst of crisis, it is essential that we understand how God deals with nations.

B. We must also understand how God deals differently with individuals and nations. Misunderstanding this core principle can lead to great confusion. Individuals can experience great mercy, joy, salvation, and healing from the great heart of God even while he is simultaneously judging their nation.

C. God has set a pattern in how he deals with nations even under the new covenant. If a nation is not under the blood of Jesus and walking in agreement with the Lord's precepts, God will pour out temporal judgments in order to awaken them to repentance. The Lord always starts by shaking the financial systems in order to wake up a nation. His last resort is military crisis that can ultimately scatter the nation.

D. In Leviticus 26, God describes this pattern of his dealings clearly.

E. So, to answer the question of whether a crisis is from God or the enemy, the answer is yes to both! Even creation is groaning because of the fall, but we must be clear that God uses crisis in nations to attempt to bring the **highest number of people to the deepest level of love possible using the least severe method.** Temporal judgments are ultimately an expression of mercy in judgments. The scriptures clearly teach, however, that God judges nations (even in the New Testament), and that his last resort is great military crisis.

There were present at that season some who told Him about the Galileans whose blood Pilate had mingled with their sacrifices. And Jesus answered and said to them, "Do you suppose that these Galileans were worse sinners than all other Galileans, because they suffered such things? I tell you, no; but unless you repent you will all likewise perish. Or those eighteen on whom the tower in Siloam fell and killed them, do you think that they were worse sinners than all other men who dwelt in Jerusalem? I tell you, no; but unless you repent you will all likewise perish." (Luke 13:1-5)

F. Over and over again, God speaks this pattern through the prophets. In Leviticus 26, God gives this scenario in advance to Israel.

G. You see this pattern in the New Covenant in 70 AD when Rome sacked Jerusalem, which was judgment based on their rejection of Jesus, their Messiah. Israel was then scattered for 2,000 years.

H. God will follow this pattern of judgment at the end of the age on a global scale. He will pour out great temporal judgments while simultaneously releasing salvation to millions.

I. In our own nation, the civil war is an example. Abraham Lincoln's second inaugural address contained the following commentary:

The Almighty has his own purposes. "Woe unto the world because of offences! For it must needs be that offences come; but woe to that man by whom the offence cometh!" If we shall suppose that American Slavery is one of those offences which, in the providence of God, must needs come, but which, having continued through His appointed time, He now wills to remove, and that He gives to both North and South, this terrible war, as the woe due to those by whom the offence came, shall we discern therein any departure from those divine attributes which the believers in a Living God always ascribe to Him? Fondly do we hope—fervently do we pray—that this mighty scourge of war may speedily pass away. Yet, if God wills that it continue, until all the wealth piled by the bond-man's two hundred and fifty years of unrequited toil shall be sunk, and until every drop of blood drawn with the lash, shall be paid by another drawn with the sword, as was said three thousand years ago, so still it must be said "the judgments of the Lord, are true and righteous altogether"[17]

J. This word is very critical to understand in Fredericksburg. When Allen Hood was here, he came under a prophetic burden about our history. The only revival that we know of in Fredericksburg's history was during the Civil War. Both sides were experiencing revival in the military camps here in Fredericksburg. Then, the next day, they would proceed to kill one another.

K. The first great awakening in the 18th century, was not enough to avert the Revolutionary War. The second great awakening in the 19th century was not enough to avert the Civil War. All these revivals did was prepare many individuals for heaven.

L. We need a burden for revival in America that will bring systemic change to our nation. We can truly shape history through the lifestyle of intercession.

M. **Many times we are tempted to bolster our personal comfort with biblical principles in the hour of crisis.** In the initial shakings of crisis, we are tempted to ease our conscious and bolster our comfort with more favorable biblical principles. We must feed on the Word (including biblical principles) with an open heart so that we can hear the "now word" in the historic moment in which we live.

N. Interpreting events will differ based on context, however. We must factor biblical principles with prophetic context in a nation. For example:

---

[17] Taken from Abraham Lincoln's Second Inaugural Address.

1.   Isaiah gives two prophecies concerning two different military invasions. In chapters 36-37, Isaiah addresses the Assyrian invasion with a promise of God's deliverance of Jerusalem. Israel was to seek refuge in Jerusalem. God would deliver the city, its temple, and his people. In chapter 39, Isaiah, addressing Hezekiah's hosting the Babylonian envoy, announces that Babylon will invade the city and take its sons and the Temple treasury and articles.

2.   In Jeremiah's day, the false prophets used Is. 36-37 to bolster their position that God would protect the city and its temple from the onslaught of Nebuchadnezzar. Jeremiah warned them of their false religion and vain hope. The prophet Jeremiah called them to embrace the correct prophetic interpretation and give themselves up to Nebuchadnezzar.

O.   Josiah gave a warning to our generation. His generation was unable to establish a culture of intercession that changed the society and averted crisis. By the time Jeremiah came, it was too late. They missed their window to bring systemic change through intercession.

1. 640-620 B.C. – Joel, Habakkuk, Zephaniah Announce the Day of the Lord

2. 640 B.C. – Josiah's Reign

3. 632 B.C. – Josiah Seeks the God of his father David

4. 628 B.C. – Josiah Purges the High Places and Idolatry Begins

5. 627 B.C. – Jeremiah the Prophet Prophesies Impending Military Judgment

6. 622 B.C. – Josiah Discovers and Restores Temple, Discovers the Law Books, and Restores True Worship.

7. 622 B.C. – Josiah Repents and Seeks the Prophetic Word from Huldah the Prophetess

Then she answered them, "Thus says the LORD God of Israel, 'Tell the man who sent you to Me, "Thus says the LORD: 'Behold, I will bring calamity on this place and on its inhabitants, all the curses that are written in the book which they have read before the king of Judah, because they have forsaken Me and burned incense to other gods, that they might provoke Me to anger with all the works of their hands. Therefore My wrath will be poured out on this place, and not be quenched.'"' But as for the king of Judah, who sent you to inquire of the LORD, in this manner you shall speak to him, 'Thus says the LORD God of Israel: "Concerning the words which you have heard --because your heart was tender, and you humbled yourself before God when you heard His words against this place and against its inhabitants, and you humbled yourself before Me, and you tore your clothes and wept before Me, I also have heard you," says the LORD. (2 Chronicles 34:23-27)

8. 609 B.C. Josiah Dies and Idolatry Takes Root

9. 605 B.C. Nebuchadnezzar Invades Judah and the Exile Begins

IV. JOEL'S FIRST TRUMPET

Blow the trumpet in Zion, and sound an alarm in My holy mountain! Let all the inhabitants of the land tremble; for the day of the LORD is coming, for it is at hand…(Joel 2:1)

A. God commands the prophet to blow two trumpets in chapter 2. This is God's primary strategy for any nation in a time of crisis.

B. The first trumpet (or prophetic message) is a bold warning about the Day of the Lord.

C. The term "Day of the Lord" refers to BOTH national scenarios of judgment and awakening, and the ultimate eschatological Day of the Lord on a global scale.

D. God is raising up messengers that will have clarity about the hour in which we live and will prophesy boldly both the terrible and glorious dimensions of the impending Day of the Lord.

For the day of the LORD is great and very terrible; who can endure it? (Joel 2:11)

E. God literally calls the prophet to sound an alarm. This is disruptive and inconvenient. Have you ever heard an alarm? It is extremely unpleasant. Though unpleasant, God's alarm serves a very important function as an expression of his great mercy.

V. JOEL'S SECOND TRUMPET

Blow the trumpet in Zion, consecrate a fast, call a sacred assembly;
gather the people, sanctify the congregation, assemble the elders, gather the
children and nursing babes; let the bridegroom go out from his chamber, and the
bride from her dressing room. Let the priests, who minister to the LORD, weep
between the porch and the altar; let them say, "Spare Your people, O LORD, and do
not give Your heritage to reproach, that the nations should rule over them. Why
should they say among the peoples, 'Where is their God?'" (Joel 2:15-17)

A.   Joel's second trumpet (prophetic message) is to gather in prayer and fasting and
      repentance.

B.   This is God's remedy. Joel gives us a glorious hope in verse 14.

      Who knows if He will turn and relent, and leave a blessing behind Him (Joel
      2:14)

C.   Corporate, prayer and fasting is always the first and central response in crisis.

      When Solomon had finished praying, fire came down from heaven and
      consumed the burnt offering and the sacrifices; and the glory of the LORD
      filled the temple. And the priests could not enter the house of the LORD,
      because the glory of the LORD had filled the LORD's house. When all the
      children of Israel saw how the fire came down, and the glory of the LORD on
      the temple, they bowed their faces to the ground on the pavement....

      ...Then the LORD appeared to Solomon by night, and said to him: "I have
      heard your prayer, and have chosen this place for Myself as a house of
      sacrifice. When I shut up heaven and there is no rain, or command the
      locusts to devour the land, or send pestilence among My people, if My people
      who are called by My name will humble themselves, and pray and seek My face,
      and turn from their wicked ways, then I will hear from heaven, and will forgive
      their sin and heal their land. Now My eyes will be open and My ears attentive
      to prayer made in this place. (2 Chronicles 7:1-3; 12-15)

D.   God promises to pour out his Spirit in response to this kind of prayer.

      And it shall come to pass afterward that I will pour out My Spirit on all
      flesh; your sons and your daughters shall prophesy (Joel 2:28)

Session 10: Apostolic Intercession – Pauline Burden and the Release of Laborers

I. THE GREAT NEED: APOSTOLIC LEADERSHIP

A. There is a crisis of spiritual leadership in the land. In America, we have many amazing spiritual fathers and mothers, but there is a crisis in many leaders as to where and *how spiritual authority functions.*

B. "Apostolic" simply means that which is sent from heaven. It speaks of that which heaven is endorsing with power. It is divine burden and divine assignment, which is backed by divine power and authority. There is no striving to impress men in apostolic ministry. It is rooted in friendship with the heavenly Bridegroom. In fact, it is often despised by men.

C. Though there are many ministries that are growing, the Lord is seeking to restore true apostolic ministry. Growth that simply comes through a personality, a popular message, marketing strategies, or entertainment will not last in the great shaking that is coming. We need that which is born of the Spirit and sent from heaven. The only key to real spiritual authority is priestly ministry (drawing near to the glory of God, ministry to the Lord, and intercession).

D. The coming shift in leadership will be a restoration of the "friends of the Bridegroom." These "friends" are leaders that will stand and hear the Bridegroom. They will lead out of a place of authority and revelation. They will delight at the Bridegroom's voice more than their own, and this will be the great joy and labor of their life: giving Jesus his bride. These men and women do not use their platform to point to themselves or build themselves, but to be nothing and that Christ would be everything.

He who has the bride is the bridegroom; but the friend of the bridegroom, who <u>*stands and hears him, rejoices greatly because of the bridegroom's voice.*</u> *Therefore this joy of mine is fulfilled. (John 3:29)*

E. These leaders will be "shepherds after God's own heart." In other words, they will stand in the council of the Lord and shepherd the people with God's heart, experience His emotions, and carry the word of the Lord.

And I will give you shepherds according to My heart, who will feed you with knowledge and understanding. (Jeremiah 3:15)

F. Our great need is for true spiritual fathers and mothers. A spiritual father or mother can be 15 years old or 55 years old (though the sphere of influence will differ). True fathers are rare.

My little children, for whom I labor in birth again until Christ is formed in you (Galatians 4:19)

But as my beloved children I warn you. For though you might have ten thousand instructors in Christ, yet you do not have many fathers; for in Christ Jesus I have begotten you through the gospel. (1 Corinthians 4:14-15)

G. Only spiritual fathers and mothers give birth to children. Only that which is "birthed" will remain. Lasting spiritual fruit comes through union with the Bridegroom, through fellowship with the Spirit.

1. Even today, we have the same issues as in the Apostle Paul's day. Many ministries are focused on building their reputations and influence, but not on giving birth to children supernaturally and then fathering them.

2. The very definition of leadership in the Kingdom of God is servanthood. Intercession is a labor of servanthood in partnership with the Holy Spirit.

    But Jesus called them to Himself and said, "You know that the rulers of the Gentiles lord it over them, and those who are great exercise authority over them. Yet it shall not be so among you; but whoever desires to become great among you, let him be your servant. And whoever desires to be first among you, let him be your slave — just as the Son of Man did not come to be served, but to serve, and to give His life a ransom for many." (Matthew 20:25- 28)

3. Jesus modeled this leadership perfectly. All authority over others in the Kingdom involves laying down your life completely on their behalf. This results in spiritual fruit that is eternal.

Let this mind be in you which was also in Christ Jesus, who, being in the form of God, did not consider it robbery to be equal with God, but made Himself of no reputation, taking the form of a bondservant, and coming in the likeness of men. And being found in appearance as a man, He humbled Himself and became obedient to the point of death, even the death of the cross. Therefore God also has highly exalted Him and given Him the name which is above every name, that at the name of Jesus every knee should bow, of those in heaven, and of those on earth, and of those under the earth, and that every tongue should confess that Jesus Christ is Lord, to the glory of God the Father. (Philippians 2:5-11)

II.   APOSTOLIC INTERCESSION

A. We "give birth" in the Spirit through intercession. Spiritual fathers stand in intercession day and night and supernaturally birth sons and daughters. Paul's apostolic ministry was consumed with the spirit of prayer. He frequently speaks of laboring in prayer "day and night" for the churches.

B. Prayer, fasting, and giving is the only context in which true spiritual authority is fashioned and lasting fruit is birthed. This is the apostolic lifestyle. In this lifestyle, we receive something from heaven, which will result in a manifestation of heaven on earth. This is the nature of the apostolic.

C. Government rests on the intercessors. Spiritual authority is *always* connected to intercession. Dick Blackwell's dream.

   And He [Jesus] shall be a priest on his throne. (Zechariah 6:13)

D. It is critical that spiritual leadership learn how to "open doors" in the Spirit for sons and daughters to enter in the Kingdom. This is the key to the revival spirit.

   Pray…that God would open to us a door for the word. (Colissians 4:3)

   And I will give you the keys of the kingdom of heaven, and whatever you bind on earth will be bound in heaven, and whatever you loose on earth will be loosed in heaven. (Matthew 16:19)

E. Rees Howells called this "a gained position" of intercession. This is what George Muller called the "grace of faith." It is literally praying through to a place of prevailing faith and of a guaranteed answer:

"Mr. Howells would often speak of the 'gained position of intercession,' and the truth of it is obvious on many occasions in his life…The price is paid, the obedience fulfilled, the inner wrestling and groanings take their full coarse, and then the 'word of the Lord comes'. 'Greater works are done.'"[18]

F. Even Jesus was instructed to ask. Right now, Jesus is constantly engaged in intercession. To be in fellowship with Christ within us and to be conformed to his image, is to become an intercessor since he is currently engaged in intercession day and night.

Ask of me, and I will make the nations your inheritance and the ends of the earth your possession. (Psalm 2:8)

Therefore He is also able to save to the uttermost those who come to God through Him, since <u>He always lives to make intercession for them</u>. (Hebrews 7:25)

G. The Pharisees' lack of authority was because they were not intercessors. They did not have fellowship with the Holy Spirit. They had tremendous knowledge of the Scriptures, but they did not embrace the intimacy and servanthood of intercession. Therefore, they had no authority, and instead of opening doors for the masses, they actually kept the masses out of the kingdom because of spiritual pride and ambition.

But woe to you, scribes and Pharisees, hypocrites! For you shut up the <u>kingdom of heaven against men</u>; for you neither go in yourselves, nor do you you allow those who are entering to go in. (Matthew 23:13)

H. This is a terrifying rebuke! The opposite of intercession is the control spirit (using people to build your personal agenda and reputation).

III. HISTORICAL INTERCESSORS: OPENING DOORS IN THE SPIRIT

A. Rees Howells

1. Rees Howells, born in South Wales in 1879, was sovereignly apprehended by the Holy Spirit and called to a radical life of intercession, Nazirite consecration, and revival.

---

[18] Grubb, Norman. "Rees Howells Intercessor." CLC Pub. 1952. P. 97.

2. At one time in his life, Rees Howells was asked by the Holy Spirit to pray without ceasing, to not wear his hat outside (at the time, a cultural embarrassment), to fast on only two meals of rice and soup every day, to turn his church over to his right hand man, and become this other leader's greatest intercessor, praying that the church would be more successful under the new leader's leadership. On top of all this, he spent three hours every night (after a long day of work in a coal mine) in prayer.

3. Rees Howells said the following of his hidden life of intercession during this season:

    *"The fellowship I had had with the Lord Himself surpassed all I ever had with man; also I had not finished going through the Bible with the Holy Spirit. **The hardest thing in my life had become the sweetest.**"*[19]

4. Rees Howells began to die totally to man-pleasing and the flesh and he began to give himself completely to intercession and intimacy. He "won" many victories, and he became known as in his region as the "man who had the Holy Ghost." Often, God would lead him to pray for someone's salvation or healing and he would "pray it through" until he was in a place of faith and he would see amazing miracles. This included the hardest "tramps" being totally saved and delivered.

B. Frank Bartleman

1. Frank Bartleman was an intercessor who lived in Los Angeles at the beginnging of the twentieth century and was part of the Azusa Street outpouring. Intercession birthed Azusa Street. Bartleman is best understood by his own words:

---

[19] *Ibid,* p. 141

"By this time the spirit of intercession had so possessed me that I prayed almost day and night. I fasted much also, until my wife almost despaired of my life at times. The sorrows of my Lord had gripped me. I was in Gethsemane with Him....At times I was afraid that I might not live to see the answers to my prayers and tears for revival. But He assured me, sending more than one angel to strengthen me."[20]

"My life by this time was literally swallowed up in prayer. I was praying day and night."[21]

"I would lie on my bed in the daytime and roll and groan under the burden. At night I could scarcely sleep for the spirit of prayer...at one time I was in such travail for nearly twenty-four hours without remission."[22]

*"It is very easy to choose second best. The prayer life is needed much more than buildings or organizations. These are often substitutes for the other. **Souls are born into the kingdom only through prayer**."[23]*

2. Bartleman's intercession, along with a community of others in Los Angeles, resulted in the greatest outpouring of the Spirit in the twentieth century, known as the Azusa Street revival. The cloud of the glory of God filled Azusa Street for three years. Creative miracles were commonplace and many souls were saved. We are benefiting from this revival to this day as arguably the greatest missions movement in history was birthed.

C. David Brainerd

1. David Brainerd was a missionary during the first great awakening in the 1700s. He gave his life in obscurity to the Native American peoples in the forests of New England. During his missionary activities, he experienced a move of the Spirit among the Native American peoples that resulted in many conversions and whole villages coming under the power of the God. He gave birth to sons and daughters.

---

[20] Bartleman, Frank. "Azusa Street" Whitaker House pub. 1982. p. 27.

[21] *Ibid.* p. 15.

[22] *Ibid.* p. 30.

[23] *Ibid.* p. 29.

2. He died at a young age of 29 from tuberculosis.

3. David Brainerd's diary has impacted thousands of the most significant leaders in the missions movement. His own words still impact us today:

   "But now, my soul more frequently desires to die to be with Christ. Oh, that my soul was rapt up in divine love, and my longing for God increased." [24]

   "God enabled me to so agonize in prayer that I was quite wet with perspiration, though in the shade and the cool wind. My soul was drawn out very much for the world, for the multitude of souls."[25]

4. The results of his intercession and preaching were profound. In his own words:

   "I stood amazed at the influence that seized the audience almost universally, and could compare it to nothing more aptly than the irresistible force of a mighty torrent, or a swelling deluge…almost all persons of all ages were bowed down."[26]

   "They were almost universally praying and crying for mercy, in every part of the house, and many out of the doors, and numbers could neither go nor stand. I had not discoursed long before their concern rose to a great degree, and the house was filled with cries and groans…" [27]

D. Daniel Nash

1. "Father Nash" was an intercessor that lived in obscurity and was in partnership with Charles Finney in the second Great Awakening. Finney's ministry was known to have an 80% success rate of conversions that lasted. This fruitfulness was birthed through the intercession of Father Nash. He is one of the great heroes of the faith.

---

[24] *The Life and Dairy of David Brainerd.* Ed. Jonathan Edwards. Grand Rapids: Baker Books. 1989. p. 12

[25] *Ibid.* p. 80-81.

[26] *Ibid.* p. 216.

[27] *Ibid.* p. 265.

2. Nash was a nameless, faceless intercessor in his generation. No pictures of him can be found. No books have been written about him. Even his descendants cannot be located.

3. Finney would send Nash to an area that he was planning to visit weeks before his arrival to prepare in deep intercession.

4. Finney's account of Nash's intercession:

   "On one occasion when I got to town to start a revival, a lady contacted me who ran a boarding house. She said, 'Brother Finney, do you know Father Nash? He and two other men have been at my boarding house for the last three days, but they haven't eaten a bite of food. I opened the door and peeped in at them because I could hear them groaning, and I saw them down on their faces. They have been this way for three days, lying prostrate on the floor and groaning. I thought something awful must have happened to them. I was afraid to go in and I didn't know what to do. Would you please come and see about them?'

   'No, it isn't necessary,' Finney replied. 'They just have a spirit of travail in prayer.'"

IV. SEPARATED TO THE HOLY SPIRIT: SENDING COMMUNITIES

A. Acts 13 gives us the apostolic pattern for revival, authority, and fruitfulness. The church at Antioch demonstrated the pattern of the early church, which was repeated in various contexts throughout the first century (see Acts 1, 2, 4, etc.).

   Now in the church that was at Antioch there were certain prophets and teachers: Barnabas, Simeon who was called Niger, Lucius of Cyrene, Manaen who had been brought up with Herod the tetrarch, and Saul. As they ministered to the Lord and fasted, the Holy Spirit said, "Now separate to Me Barnabas and Saul for the work to which I have called them." Then, having fasted and prayed, and laid hands on them, they sent them away. (Acts 13:1-3)

   And all these were devoting themselves to prayer....When the day of Pentecost arrived, they were all in one place. And suddenly there came from heaven, a sound like a mighty rushing wind....and there were added that day about three thousand souls. (Acts 1:14-2:41)

And they devoted themselves to the apostles teaching and fellowship, to the breaking of bread and prayers. And awe came over every soul... (Acts 2:42-43)

And when they had prayed, the place where they were gathered together was shaken, and they were all filled with the Holy Spirit and continued to speak the word of God with boldness. (Acts 4:31)

B. The church of Antioch was probably quite comfortable in their church growth. They were the revival center of the whole world at the time. They were the furthest the gospel had gone from Jerusalem. They had profound prophetic ministry and teachers functioning in unity. It was an apostolic community.

C. Undoubtedly, with the memory of Acts 1-4 still fresh in their mind, they understood that in order to continue to experience apostolic expansion and the open heavens, ministry to the Lord (worship) and prayer were necessary. They may have been only thinking about keeping the revival of Antioch flourishing and growing; the Holy Spirit, however, had apostolic assignments on his heart.

D. In the context of corporate prayer and fasting, the Holy Spirit commissioned Paul and Barnabas on their first missionary journey, which we are still benefiting from to this day.

E. To be a part of an apostolic community is to be a part of something that is bigger than us, divinely led, supernatural, and impossible to orchestrate by human ingenuity. This is always birthed in corporate ministry to the Lord and prayer and fasting.

F. As Andrew Murray says:

"We have the key that can unlock the dungeon of atheism and of heathendom. But, oh! we are more occupied with our work than we are with prayer. We believe more in speaking to men than we believe in speaking to God."[28]

G. Oh that we would believe more in speaking to God than to men! How often we have plowed forward in our wisdom, our strength and our timing. There is sweet fellowship that is available to us – the Holy Spirit doing part of the work and men doing the other part.

---

[28] Murray, Andrew. "Absolute Surrender". Lampost Pub. 2009. P. 43

H.   This is God's global strategy for evangelism of every nation: communities of prayer and fasting that birth apostolic laborers.

Then He said to His disciples, "The harvest truly is plentiful, but the laborers are few. Therefore pray the Lord of the harvest to send out laborers into His harvest." (Matthew 9:27-28)

V.   PAUL: MODEL INTERCESSOR

A.   The Apostle Paul was a model of intercession and apostolic ministry. As mentioned above, he was supernaturally commissioned by the Holy Spirit through the church at Antioch in the context of an ongoing prayer meeting with fasting.

B.   Paul was a man of constant prayer. His authority flowed from perpetual communion with the Beloved. He addressed the reality of intercession in nearly all of his writings. He instructed the churches to "always pray." He described his personal life of intercession as "constant," "without ceasing," "night and day," and "praying always" (Eph. 1:16, Rom 1:10, Phil. 1:3-4, I Cor.1:4, I Thess. 1:3, 3:10). He asked for intercession from the church regularly. He even wrote out intercessory prayers in most of his epistles!

C.   This kind of prayer was the central expression of his role as the "father" of the churches that he planted.

D.   The other Apostles were also known as men of prayer. James, the Just, who was the brother of Jesus, wrote the book of James and was the senior apostolic leader of the church in Jerusalem in the first century. He was such a profound intercessor that there were indentations on the floor next to his bed where he would kneel for hours in prayer everyday!

E.   Paul literally carried the churches in his heart day and night before the Lord. He describes this intercessory burden as "anguish." Paul was in the anguish of intercession over the churches and specific individuals. Below are just a few examples:

....without ceasing I mention you always in my prayers... (Romans 1:10)

...I remember you constantly in my prayers night and day. (2 Timothy 1:3)

Therefore I also, after I heard of your faith in the Lord Jesus and your love for all the saints, do not cease to give thanks for you, making mention of you in my prayers (Ephesians 1:15-16)

For this reason we also, since the day we heard it, do not cease to pray for you (Colossians 1:9)

...my little children, for whom I am again in the anguish of childbirth until Christ is formed in you! (Galatians 4:19)

...besides the other things [tribulations], what comes upon me daily: my deep concern for all the churches. (2 Corinthians 11:28)

I thank my God upon every remembrance of you, always in every prayer of mine making request for you all with joy (Philippians 1:3-4)

....be constant in prayer. (Romans 12:12)

praying at all times in the Spirit, with all prayer and supplication. To that end keep alert with all perseverance, making supplication for all the saints (Ephesians 6:18)

pray without ceasing (1 Thessalonians 5:17)

F.   Says E.M. Bounds:

"Paul was a leader by appointment and by universal recognition and acceptance. He had many mighty forces in his ministry. His conversion, so conspicuous and

radical, was a great force, a perfect magazine of aggressive and defensive
warfare...but these forces were not the divinest of energies which brought forth
the largest results to his ministry. Paul's course was more distinctly shaped and
his rendered more powerfully successful by prayer than by any other force."[29]

VI. PAUL'S ULTIMATE BURDEN

A.   Paul's ultimate burden was the salvation of Israel. This is not simply because
     Paul was a Jew, but because he understood the purposes and glory of God. Paul
     understood that the fullness of Gentiles being saved and the Gentile church
     coming to fullness would result in Israel's salvation.

*Brethren, my heart's desire and prayer to God for Israel is that they may be
saved. (Romans 10:1)*

*I say then, have they stumbled that they should fall? Certainly not! But
through their fall, to provoke them to jealousy, salvation has come to the
Gentiles. Now if their fall is riches for the world, and their failure riches for
the Gentiles, how much more their fullness! For I speak to you Gentiles;
inasmuch as I am an apostle to the Gentiles, I magnify my ministry, if by any
means I may provoke to jealousy those who are my flesh and save some of them.
For if their being cast away is the reconciling of the world, what will their
acceptance be but life from the dead? (Romans 11:11-15)*

*For I do not desire, brethren, that you should be ignorant of this mystery, lest
you should be wise in your own opinion, that blindness in part has happened to
Israel until the fullness of the Gentiles has come in. And so all Israel will be
saved. (Romans 11:25-26)*

B.   Paul went further than human sympathy for Israel. He entered into Jesus'
     emotions for the salvation of Israel. God burns with passion for Israel's complete
     restoration.

---

[29] Bounds, E.M. *The Complete Works of E.M. Bounds on Prayer* (Grand Rapids, MI: Baker Books, 1990), p. 544.

For I could wish that I myself were accursed from Christ for my brethren, my countrymen according to the flesh (Romans 9:3)

O Jerusalem, Jerusalem, the one who kills the prophets and stones those who are sent to her! How often I wanted to gather your children together, as a hen gathers her chicks under her wings, but you were not willing! See! Your house is left to you desolate; for I say to you, you shall see Me no more till you say, "Blessed is He who comes in the name of the LORD!" (Matthew 23:37- 39)

I am zealous for Jerusalem and for Zion with great zeal. (Zechariah 1:14)

C.   At the end of the age, God will raise up millions of Gentile believers that will pray for Israel's salvation. This intercession will result in all of Israel being saved and fully restored.

I have set watchmen on your walls, O Jerusalem; They shall never hold their peace day or night. You who make mention of the LORD, do not keep silent, and give Him no rest till He establishes and till He makes Jerusalem a praise in the earth. (Isaiah 62:6-7)

D.   Personal journey into intercession for Israel. One of my most significant prophetic experiences was related to prayer for Israel. This is a clear mandate over this house.

Session 11 – Forerunners: Eschatological Priestly Ministry

The voice of one crying in the wilderness: "Prepare the way of the LORD; make straight in the desert a highway for our God…The glory of the LORD shall be revealed, and all flesh shall see it together." (Isaiah 40:3-5)

I. INTRODUCTION TO THE FORERUNNER MINISTRY

A. One of our core mandates at the Fredericksburg Prayer Furnace is to minister with a "forerunner spirit." On a personal level, the first prophetic word I ever received, while still in my mother's womb, was related to my calling to the forerunner ministry. This was long before this idea was being talked about on wider scale in the Body of Christ. I have since come to understand this unique ministry which is critical for transitional generations. I am confident that I am to give the rest of my life to raise up forerunners that will prepare many for the greatest hour of human history.

B. The forerunner ministry is a unique expression of prophetic ministry. Forerunners are messengers that prepare the way for the coming of the Lord in great revival, judgment, and the time frame of Jesus' return. The forerunner ministry is a prophetic ministry in the context of a ***transitional generation.***

C. Transitional generations are specific time frames leading up to a "Day of the Lord" reality. When the scriptures use the term "Day of the Lord," it is referring to a period time, which embodies the characteristics of the eschatological (end-times) Day of the Lord. Forerunners begin to experience what God is about to release across the nations just a ***small step ahead*** of the rest of the Body of Christ. Thus, they become voices with clarity to prepare the people.

D. Forerunners prepare the way of the Lord by preparing people to respond rightly to the Lord in a time of intensity. Forerunners boldly speak of the urgency of the hour in which they live and events which are about to transpire. The message of the forerunner is the revelation of Jesus that is about to be expressed globally.

E. Their message is not just that, in fact, an hour of crisis is coming, but why it is coming. What is on the Lord's heart? Why is he shaking the nations? Forerunners prepare and interpret the crisis to the Body of Christ and the nations.

F.   I believe that we are in the beginning stages of the Day of the Lord in a real sense. I believe that there may be people alive on the earth that will witness the second coming of Jesus.

G.   We are in the beginning of the "birth pangs" of the second coming of Jesus.

For many will come in my name, saying, "I am the Christ," and they will lead many astray. And you will hear of wars and rumors of wars. See that you are not alarmed, for this must take place, but the end is not yet. For nation will rise against nation, and kingdom against kingdom, and there will be famines and earthquakes in various places. All these are but the beginning of the birth pains. (Matthew 24:5-8)

H.   Every time we enter a transitional generation, of which we are currently in the beginning stages, God must raise up voices. This is his mercy strategy. He did it in the generation of Jesus' first coming through John the Baptist and he will do it in the generation of his second coming.

Behold, I will send you Elijah the prophet before the coming of the great and dreadful day of the LORD. And he will turn the hearts of the fathers to the children, and the hearts of the children to their fathers, lest I come and strike the earth with a curse. (Malachi 4:5-6)

I.   Isaiah 40 speaks of the activity of the Holy Spirit at a specific time frame: the generation of the Lord's return. Though John the Baptist embodied a partial fulfillment of this prophecy in the first century, there is an even greater fulfillment in the final generation. There are real, nameless, faceless voices that the Holy Spirit is preparing in this time.

"Comfort, yes, comfort My people!" says your God. "Speak comfort to Jerusalem, and cry out to her, that her warfare is ended, that her iniquity is pardoned; for she has received from the Lord's hand double for all her sins." The voice of one crying in the wilderness: "Prepare the way of the Lord; make straight in the desert a highway for our God. Every valley shall be exalted and every mountain and hill brought low; the crooked places shall be made straight and the rough places smooth; the glory of the Lord shall be revealed, and all flesh shall see it together; for the mouth of the Lord has spoken."

The voice said, "Cry out!" And I said, "What shall I cry?" "All flesh is grass, and all its loveliness is like the flower of the field. The grass withers, the flower fades, because the breath of the Lord blows upon it; surely the people are grass. The grass withers, the flower fades, but the word of our God stands forever." O Zion, You who bring good tidings, get up into the high mountain; O Jerusalem, You who bring good tidings, lift up your voice with strength, lift it up, be not afraid; say to the cities of Judah, "Behold your God!" Behold, the Lord God shall come with a strong hand, and His arm shall rule for Him; behold, His reward is with Him, and His work before Him. He will feed His flock like a shepherd; He will gather the lambs with His arm, and carry them in His bosom, and gently lead those who are with young. (Isaiah 40:1-11)

J. This prophecy is a promise that God will raise up voices that will shepherd the church and the nations in the greatest hour of human history. Voices are those that have history, clarity of intimacy, and urgency in their secret life.

K. To be a voice requires a lifestyle – there is abandonment to God in lifestyles of prayer, fasting, and going deep in encounter and the knowledge of God now that will prepare us, to prepare others, to prepare the nations in that day.

L. How is the forerunner message a "comfort" to Israel and the people of God?

M. First, forerunners have clarity about the ***end of the story.*** They understand the wisdom of God in the shaking, and they are locked into the glory that is coming to the nations at the second coming of Jesus. Forerunners see themselves and the people of God in the story. This is true comfort.

   The voice of one crying in the wilderness…The glory of the Lord shall be revealed, and all flesh shall see it together; for the mouth of the Lord has spoken. (Isaiah 40:3,5)

N. The second comfort for the people of God through the forerunner ministry is a focus on the eternity of God. They live from heaven to earth. They live in a consciousness of God and the eternal realm. They proclaim the temporal nature of this age and the natural realm. Forerunners prophesy through their words and their lifestyles, "There is more than this! There is more than meets the eye!"

   The voice said, "Cry out!" And I said, "What shall I cry?" "All flesh is grass, and all its loveliness is like the flower of the field. The grass withers, the flower fades, because the breath of the Lord blows upon it; surely the people are grass. The grass withers, the flower fades, but the word of our God stands forever." (Isaiah 40:6-8)

O. This message of comfort is contrary to the false comfort that will be proclaimed, and already is being proclaimed. This false comfort says, "Everything is going to be fine. There will be only peace and safety." This false comfort avoids everything that is negative and leaves people unprepared.

P.   The "mountains being brought low" speaks of the forerunner ministry's focus on humility as being the central response needed in this hour. The mountains speak of that which is rooted in human arrogance. The forerunner ministry directly confronts this pride while simultaneously reaching down to the poor, the oppressed, and the humble to pull them into exaltation. This means that systems that are rooted in pride are about to shake. There will be great leadership changes in every sphere. This will manifest fully in the government of Jesus taking over every human institution.

Q.   There will be forerunners in every sphere of society: writers, preachers, singers, artists, businessmen, etc.

R.   The forerunner declares that great change is coming and that change demands preparation. Status quo will no longer suffice. God is about to visit in an unprecedented way. I believe that this will be the central calling for many people.

II.   THE GREAT AND TERRIBLE DAY

A.   There are two major facets to the Day of The Lord. It is ***great*** and it also ***very terrible***. For those in Christ, it will be a great day. Though we will experience great shaking in the natural, we will also experience great glory. For the unbelieving in the nations, it will be a very terrible day, beyond anything the world has ever seen.

*For the day of the Lord is **great** and **very terrible**; Who can endure it? (Joel 2:11)*

*Behold, I will send you Elijah the prophet before the coming of the **great** and **dreadful** day of the LORD. (Malachi 4:5)*

B.   Some streams only emphasize the *great* dimensions of the Day of the Lord. Others primarily emphasize the *terrible* dimensions without a vision for the victorious church. We must study and go deep in both dimensions.

C.   Jesus spoke of a "flute and a dance" and a "funeral dirge" in the Day of the Lord context (**Matthew 11:17**). These are two sides of one coin of the Day of the Lord.

D.   There are over 150 chapters in the Bible which have the Day of the Lord as their primary focus. God is filled with zeal for the Day of the Lord.

For the day of vengeance is in My heart... (Isaiah 63:4)

E.   The proclamation of the Day of the Lord is not primarily based on knowing information about the end-times in an intellectual, cerebral way. It is encountering the Bridegroom, King, and Judge in a personal way – seeing Jesus in the eschatological scriptures.

Session 12: The Sermon on the Mount and the Fasted Lifestyle

I.   INTRODUCTION

A.   The lifestyle of priestly ministry (accessing the Holy Place, intimacy, ministry to the Lord and intercession) is basic Christianity and is the calling of every believer. The priestly ministry is our first ministry. It is the source of our life in the Spirit and our spiritual authority to shake the nations of the earth with the reality of the kingdom of God.

Therefore, brethren, having boldness to enter the Holiest by the blood of Jesus, by a new and living way which He consecrated for us, through the veil, that is, His flesh, and having a High Priest over the house of God, let us draw near with a true heart in full assurance of faith, having our hearts sprinkled from an evil conscience and our bodies washed with pure water. Let us hold fast the confession of our hope without wavering, for He who promised is faithful. (Hebrews 10:19-23)

B.   We, like Jesus, are "born from above." We have a heavenly citizenship and a heavenly ministry. We live and think from heaven to earth, not from earth to heaven. Accessing this life in the Spirit and moving in the authority of Christ is our greatest privilege in the gospel.

Therefore, holy brethren, partakers of the heavenly calling, consider the Apostle and High Priest of our confession, Christ Jesus (Hebrews 3:1)

C.   Jesus outlines the priestly-kingly lifestyle in the Sermon the Mount (Matthew 5-7). The Sermon on the Mount is the constitution of the kingdom of God. The degree to which our ministry and our life reflects the Sermon the Mount is the degree to which we are building something that will last in the coming shakings and into the age to come. The Sermon on the Mount is the heavenly value-system and the heavenly lifestyle.

"Therefore whoever hears these sayings of Mine, and does them, I will liken him to a wise man who built his house on the rock: and the rain descended, the floods came, and the winds blew and beat on that house; and it did not fall, for it was founded on the rock. But everyone who hears these sayings of Mine, and does not do them, will be like a foolish man who built his house on the sand: and the rain descended, the floods came, and the winds blew and beat on that house; and it fell. And great was its fall." And so it was, when Jesus had ended these sayings, that the people were astonished at His teaching, for

He taught them as one having authority, and not as the scribes. (Matthew 7:24-29)

II.   THE SERMON ON THE MOUNT: THE VALUE SYSTEM OF THE KINGDOM (MATTHEW 5-7)

A.   Jesus gives the very definition of greatness in the Sermon on the Mount. Jesus intends that we live in constant fellowship with God and that we live with a vibrant heart before him. Our desire for greatness is not too strong, b ut too weak. Let us press in to be great in the sight of the Lord as Jesus defines greatness!

B.   The beatitudes reflect this heavenly value system and are at the foundation of priestly ministry. The entire teaching of the Sermon on the Mount is the outworking of these core heavenly values. This is the joyful, or the "blessed" life. All of our life in God is related to these values. Oh that these values would become the central pursuit of the church on a global scale – great revival would result.

C.   Jesus outlines six toxins that destroy the beautiful, joyful life (Matthew 5:21-48). He also outlines five positive activities that, when lived by faith, cause the beautiful life in the Spirit to bloom and flourish (prayer, fasting, giving, serving, and blessing enemies; Mt. 6:1-18). The Beatitudes are the picture of the beautiful life in the Spirit.

III.   BEATITUDES: DEFINITIONS (MATTHEW 5:3-12)

A.   *Poor in spirit* (theirs is the kingdom of heaven) – to acknowledge our great need and barrenness of soul apart from the power of the Spirit. It is to possess nothing but God. It is to lean on God in intimacy with all of our heart.

B.   *Mourning* (for they shall be comforted) – holy desperation leading to extreme pursuit of God and breakthrough in the heart. It is being touched on an emotional and intellectual level with the *reality* of our need and the need of others.

C.   *Meekness* (for they shall inherit the earth) – to use our best resources, abilities, and power to serve others without need of honor from men. Humility is to acknowledge our absolute dependence on God and to live for others first.

D.   ***Hunger and thirst for righteousness*** (for they will be filled) – radical pursuit of God in all seasons of life. It is a deep longing for the fullness of God that leads to a removal of everything that hinders breakthrough in the fullness of   God.

E.   ***Merciful*** (for they shall receive mercy) – relating to other with gentleness and compassion, even when they fail us or when they hurt us. It is expressing tenderness towards the needy.

F.   ***Pure in heart*** (for they shall see God) – breakthrough of purity (righteousness) in our thoughts, will, motives, and emotions before God. It is sincere love for what God loves and desire to see others succeed without personal gain.

G.   ***Peacemakers*** (for they shall be called sons of God) – to bring peace and healing to that which is out of God's will (relationships, sick bodies, corrupt governments).

H.   ***Persecuted for righteousness*** (for theirs is the kingdom of heaven) – enduring the response of the spirit of the age to wholehearted love for Jesus.

IV.   THE FASTED LIFESTYLE (MATTHEW 6)

A.   In Matthew 6, Jesus outlines three hidden activities (to be done in secret) that specifically enhance our ability to receive the grace of God and experience the above realities in our heart. The three secret activities are: prayer, fasting, and giving.

> *Take heed that you do not do your charitable deeds before men, to be seen by them. Otherwise you have no reward from your Father in heaven. Therefore, <u>when you do a charitable deed</u>, do not sound a trumpet before you as the hypocrites do in the synagogues and in the streets, that they may have glory from men. Assuredly, I say to you, they have their reward. ³ But when you do a charitable deed, do not let your left hand know what your right hand is doing, ⁴ that your charitable deed may be in secret; <u>and your Father who sees in secret will Himself reward you openly</u>. (Matthew 6:1-4)*

> *And <u>when you pray</u>, you shall not be like the hypocrites. For they love to pray standing in the synagogues and on the corners of the streets, that they may be seen by men. Assuredly, I say to you, they have their reward. But you, when you pray, go into your room, and when you have shut your door, pray to your Father who is in the secret place; and <u>your Father who sees in secret will reward you openly</u>. (Matthew 5:5-6)*

> *Moreover, <u>when you fast</u>, do not be like the hypocrites, with a sad countenance. For they disfigure their faces that they may appear to men to be fasting. Assuredly, I say to you, they have their reward. But you, when you fast, anoint your head and wash your face, so that you do not appear to men to be fasting, but to your Father who is in the secret place; <u>and your Father who sees in secret will reward you openly</u>. (Matthew 5:16-18)*

B. Jesus promises "open reward" from the Father for this lifestyle in the grace of God. These rewards are in this age and the age to come. Some of the rewards are external in nature (ie. breakthrough in ministry of the Spirit, answered prayer, etc.), and some of the rewards are internal in nature (ie. godly emotions, tenderizing of the heart in love, intimate encounter with God in prayer, etc). The Father cares about our fasting. He is attentive to it. This alone gives fasting unspeakable value.

C. Jesus taught this lifestyle because the rewards so far outweigh the difficulties. The reward is guaranteed from the lips of Christ himself. The guaranteed reward makes fasting very important. It provides an open door to express spiritual hunger and receive more from God.

D. Fasting in the grace of God actually produces significant change both internally and externally. Fasting begets transformation.

E. Fasting is not earning something from God through works. It is a positioning of our hearts to receive greater grace. It is intentional weakness for the purpose of spiritual strength. Fasting is a call to voluntary weakness in order to experience more of the presence and power of God.

F. Regular fasting is for every believer. Often, fasting is thought to be for the "radical" believers. In fact, the fasted lifestyle is part of Christianity 101. It is the normal Christian life.

> *"The man who never fasts is no more on his way to heaven than the man who never prays." (John Wesley)*

G. Fasting is an expression of "spiritual violence" which gives us access to the fullness of God. We give up legitimate pleasures in order to enter into the higher pleasures of God. Fasting is a great privilege! We will not be fasting in the age to come!

> *And from the days of John the Baptist until now the kingdom of heaven suffers violence, and the violent take it by force. (Matthew 11:12)*

H.   John the Baptist lived a radical fasted lifestyle in the wilderness. He was a picture of what the Lord is going to release on the church at the end of the age, preceding the second coming of Jesus. There are seasons where more intense fasting is the appropriate response to the urgency of the hour. We are in an hour of urgency right now as we approach the final generation and temporal judgments in our nation.

> *For John came neither eating nor drinking… (Matthew 11:18)*

I.   Indeed, fasting was a significant part of the lifestyle of all those who have made deep impact for the gospel. The early church fasted two days per week. The Apostle Paul speaks of "fasting often" when describing his own lifestyle (2 Cor. 11:25-27). Fasting increases grace for our priestly calling to access heavenly realities.

J.   *We, and the Christian culture in which we live, are under the delusion that we are mightily abandoned to God, but in truth most of us are spiritually stifled and dull without knowing it. A life of fasting exposes the true reality of our spiritual health by setting us down right in the torrent of our screaming souls. And what is our real estate? We cling to false pleasures and securities. We have small capacities to hear from God. We crave the approval of man. We defend our reputations. We satisfy our souls with entertainment, music, and television…the nature of fasting and prayer is that it separates us from all the "background noise" that has been concealing these realities.[30]*

K.   *The greatest enemy of hunger for God is not poison but apple pie. It is not the banquet of the wicked that dulls our appetite for heaven, but the endless nibbling at the table of the world…For all the ill that Satan can do, when God describes what keeps us from the banquet table of his love, it is a piece of land, a yoke of oxen, and a wife (Luke 14:18-20). The greatest adversary of love to God is not his enemies but his gifts. And the most deadly appetites are not for the poison of evil, but for the simple pleasures of earth. For when these replace an appetite for God himself, the idolatry is scarcely recognizable, and almost incurable.[31]*

L.   Numbers 6 speaks of a consecration that is voluntary called "the vow of the Nazirite." This reflects the Sermon on the Mount. God is raising up a new breed of Nazirites on the earth, motivated by deep love for Jesus, filled with the Spirit, and releasing reformation and revival through intercession.

---

[30] Bickle, Mike. *The Rewards of Fasting* (Kansas City, MO: Forerunner Books, 2005), p. 58)

[31] Piper, John. A *Hunger for God.* Crossway Books. 1997. p. 14.

V.   REASONS WHY WE FAST

A.   We fast in order to position ourselves to receive an *increase in the spirit of revelation*. Specifically, we receive understanding of what the Spirit is saying to the church in this hour. The prophetic spirit is connected to fasting.

Daniel…from the first day that you set your heart to understand…your words were heard; and I have come because of your words. (Daniel 10:12)

I set my face toward the Lord God to make request by prayer with fasting… While I was speaking…Gabriel…talked with me, and said, "O Daniel, I have now come forth to give you skill to understand… understand the vision…" (Daniel 9:3, 21-23)

1.   John the Baptist lived a radical fasted lifestyle (Matthew 11) as the forerunner of Jesus' first coming; so will the prophetic church in the generation of the Lord's return.

2.   The forerunner ministry requires fasting.

B.   We fast for an *increase in the power of the Spirit in ministry* (the baptism of fire).

So He said to them, "This kind can come out by nothing but prayer and fasting." (Mark 9:29)

1.   Most of the great leaders of revival and transformation embraced radical lifestyles of fasting and prayer. John G. Lake embraced radical fasting and spiritual hunger leading up to his baptism in the Holy Spirit which resulted in hundreds of thousands of supernatural healings. He boldly pursued the power of the apostolic church. Mahesh Chavda did two forty day fasts per year for 10 years. He subsequently saw the dead literally raised and whole villages in Africa being saved. The Azusa Street outpouring began in a season of corporate fasting and prayer. David Brainerd's final encouragement to young ministers of his day, while on his deathbed, was to embrace regular, secret prayer and fasting.

2.   See Addendum 3. This book launched the healing revival in the late forties as thousands of people read it and engaged in forty fasts for greater power. One year after this book was released the State of Israel was also born! Though the theology is not perfect, it was a tool to release viral fasting and prayer in this nation with unprecedented results!

C.   We fast to *stop a crisis*.

> *Blow the trumpet in Zion, consecrate a fast, call a sacred assembly;*
> *gather the people, sanctify the congregation, assemble the elders, gather*
> *the children and nursing babes; let the bridegroom go out from his chamber,*
> *and the bride from her dressing room. Let the priests, who minister to the*
> *LORD, weep between the porch and the altar; let them say, "Spare Your*
> *people, O LORD, and do not give Your heritage to reproach…" (Joel 2:15-17)*

> *Who knows if He will turn and relent, and leave a blessing behind Him (Joel*
> *2:14)*

D.   We fast to *release a governmental shift in nations.* We shape history through prayer and fasting.

> *In the first year of Darius the son of Ahasuerus, of the lineage of the Medes,*
> *who was made king over the realm of the Chaldeans— in the first year of his*
> *reign I, Daniel, understood by the books the number of the years specified by*
> *the word of the LORD through Jeremiah the prophet, that He would*
> *accomplish seventy years in the desolations of Jerusalem. Then I set my face*
> *toward the Lord God to make request by prayer and supplications, with fasting,*
> *sackcloth, and ashes….(Daniel 9:1-3)*

> *Then he said to me, "Do not fear, Daniel, for from the first day that you set*
> *your heart to understand, and to humble yourself before your God, your words*
> *were heard; and I have come because of your words. But the prince of the*
> *kingdom of Persia withstood me twenty-one days" (Daniel 10:12-13)*

1.   The prophetic destinies of nations must be contended for, not simply assumed. Daniel is our model.

E.   We fast to *cultivate self-control and restraint* related to the pleasures of this age.

1.   The reason that many at the end of the age will fall into apostasy is related to lawlessness, which flows from the appetites of the flesh gaining dominance.

> *And because lawlessness will abound, the love of many will grow cold.*
> *(Matthew 24:12)*

2. The love of food was the main reason that the children of Israel wanted to return to Israel after Moses led them out into the wilderness. They desired the food of Egypt more than the Promised Land! The issue was not starvation but "tasty food!"

Now the mixed multitude who were among them yielded to intense craving; so the children of Israel also wept again and said: "Who will give us meat to eat? We remember the fish which we ate freely in Egypt, the cucumbers, the melons, the leeks, the onions, and the garlic; but now our whole being is dried up; there is nothing at all except this manna before our eyes!" (Numbers 11:4-6)

But I discipline my body and bring it into subjection, lest, when I have preached to others, I myself should become disqualified. (1 Corinthians 9:27)

F. We fast to grow in our experience of *intimacy with Jesus and his manifest presence*.

Then the disciples of John came to Him, saying, "Why do we and the Pharisees fast often, but Your disciples do not fast?" And Jesus said to them, "Can the friends of the Bridegroom <u>mourn</u> as long as the Bridegroom is with them? But the days will come when the Bridegroom will be taken away from them, and <u>then they will fast</u>." (Matthew 9:14-15)

1. John's disciples were asking about Jesus' ability to produce dedication. Jesus' answer to their question on fasting is the greatest teaching on fasting in the NT.

2. Jesus acknowledged that the disciples had no need of mourning and fasting when he was present with them, but when he "was taken" from them in his death, resurrection, and ascension, fasting would be a part of their lifestyle. This fasting would be motivated, not by any religious obligation, but by *desire for the Bridegroom's presence*.

3. Jesus established the New Covenant through his death and resurrection, by which the Spirit would dwell in each believer. Fasting would then take on a whole new dimension because the depths of God would be revealed to his disciples by the indwelling Spirit (1 Cor. 2:10; Heb. 10:19-22).

4. This type of fasting tenderizes the heart to receive, more quickly and deeply, the revelation of the love of Christ and his beauty. It produces fascination. It delivers us from our terminal boredom.

5.   This "Bridegroom fast" changes our desires. The Word of God becomes alive as we fast. Prophetic dreams increase. Our awareness of the Holy Spirit's presence within us increases.

6.   As we feel God more, our identity as sons and daughters is strengthened.

VI.   CONCLUSION

A.   We encourage people to fast at least one day per week. Two days per week is better.

B.   People who are pregnant, nursing, or have health problems should consult their doctors before fasting.

C.   The level at which a person engages in fasting from food should be determined according to age and with regard to any physical limitations. Those with a known or suspected physical disability or illness, or with any history of an eating disorder, should *never* fast except in consultation with (and under the supervision of) a qualified physician.

D.   Fasting is actually healthy!

E.   Minors are discouraged from fasting food and should *never* engage in even a partial fast without parental consent and oversight.

F.   Fasting is always voluntary. There is no biblical commandment which regulates how much one should fast. This opens us up to even greater degrees of abandonment to God!

VII.   FIVE TYPES OF FASTING FOOD

1. The ***regular fast*** is going without food and drinking only water or that which has no calories.

2. The ***liquid fast*** is going without solid food and drinking only light liquids (like fruit juices).

3. The ***partial fast***, or Daniel fast, abstains from tasty foods and eats only vegetables or nuts, etc.

4. The ***Benedict Fast***, established by Saint Benedict (525 AD), consists of only one meal a day.

5. The ***absolute fast***, or Esther fast, abstains from food and water (Esth. 4:16). Exercise caution!

Where there is no prophetic vision the people cast off restraint... (Proverbs 29:18 ESV)

Where there is no vision, the people perish... (Proverbs 29:18 KJV)

I.   THE POWER OF VISION

    A.   Prophetic vision is one of the most powerful forces in life. Vision drives all that we do. We are all living according to someone's vision for our lives, either God's or someone else's. Even Starbucks has a vision for you.

    B.   In the vacuum of prophetic vision, people live without restraint and ultimately perish. There is great danger in passivity regarding understanding our prophetic destiny.

    C.   Our life vision (or calling) comes from the Lord by a spirit of revelation (Eph. 1:15-18). This vision will sustain and carry you in the midst of dark seasons and success.

        For this reason we also, since the day we heard it, do not cease to pray for you, and to ask that you may be filled with the knowledge of His will in all wisdom and spiritual understanding (Colossians 1:9)

    D.   "Prophets are forged in the wilderness." (Lou Engle)

II.   BIRTHING OF VISION

    A.   There is a process by which we come into an understanding of our prophetic destiny. This process often involves pursuit, prayer, and fasting.

        Father of glory, may give to you the spirit of wisdom and revelation in the knowledge of Him, the eyes of your understanding being enlightened; that <u>you may know what is the hope of His calling</u>...(Ephesians 1:17-18)

    B.   "Lose yourself and check-in in 25 years."

    C.   What makes your heart alive in God?

D.   The role of the prophetic is important in this process. Words from others are primarily for the purpose of confirmation. Most often, God desires to speak to you personally, though he will also use those in the office of the prophet to confirm callings and destinies at strategic times.

III.   DEATH OF THE VISION

A.   Often, the Lord creates circumstances that make your prophetic vision look totally impossible. He effectively kills the vision for your own protection. Your prophetic destiny is bigger than you. It is not something that you can accomplish in your own strength and ability. The Lord has to pry your hands of the very gift that he desires to give you.

B.   The Lord is filled with zeal that he would continue to be your first reward. Prophetic vision is simply partnership with him. It is an expression of intimacy with him that absolutely requires a vital connection to him.

C.   In our zeal for our prophetic vision, we can quickly lose the plot, as it were, in our intimacy with Christ.

D.   This process of the dealings of the Holy Spirit in our immaturity keeps our pride from being energized. We quickly lose any hope in our own abilities to accomplish our God-given calling.

E.   The Lord is committed to making us worthy to not end up in judgment.

F.   Walking worthy = the measure of meekness equals the measure of calling.

I, therefore, the prisoner of the Lord, beseech you to walk worthy of the calling with which you were called, with all lowliness and gentleness, with longsuffering, bearing with one another in love. (Ephsians 4:1-2)

Who is wise and understanding among you? Let him show by good conduct that his works are done in the meekness of wisdom. But if you have bitter envy and self-seeking in your hearts, do not boast and lie against the truth. This wisdom does not descend from above, but is earthly, sensual, demonic. For where envy and self-seeking exist, confusion and every evil thing are there. But the wisdom that is from above is first pure, then peaceable, gentle, willing to yield, full of mercy and good fruits, without partiality and without hypocrisy. Now the fruit of righteousness is sown in peace by those who make peace. (James 3:13-18)

G.   If you receive true prophetic vision, get ready for surprising times of mistreatment and delay.

An inheritance gained hastily at the beginning will not be blessed at the end. (Proverbs 20:21)

1.   David received prophetic vision for his role in redemptive history when Samuel anointed him as the next king of Israel. (1 Sam. 16)

2.   This was followed by 13 years of persecution and threats of murder from the demonized King Saul before he was made king of Israel.

3.   Saul was David's seminary. He learned meekness and love for God, which enabled him to avoid becoming another Saul when he was king.

4.   David's worst enemy was not Saul. It was David.

5.   Joseph modeled this same phenomenon. He received his prophetic destiny in dreams about 13 years before any kind of fulfillment. He, too, suffered years of mistreatment in the process.

6.   Mistreatment is our great gift from God.

H.   The inheritance we are laboring for will harm us if we get it too soon. Many good men have been casualties of the anointing of the Holy Spirit.

I.   We need endurance and patience.

And we desire that each one of you show the same diligence to the full assurance of hope until the end, that you do not become sluggish, but imitate those who through faith and patience inherit the promises. (Hebrews 6:11-12)

IV.   FULLNESS OF VISION

A.   God will release the fullness of all he has promised you. There are often seasons of partial fulfillment of prophetic vision before the fullness.

B.   This age is ultimately only the very initial fulfillment of our prophetic calling. There is a dynamic continuity between this age and the age to come.

C. Our assignment in the Millennial Kingdom, and the New Heavens and the New Earth, is our ultimate calling. We are simply in preparation for that fuller manifestation of our destiny.

D. There are very significant assignments in this age, which will come to fruition as we are faithful.

E. Prophetic vision will require hard work to come into fullness.

V. COMPONENTS OF A FOCUSED LIFE

A. **Overall life vision** – primary purpose in life; one sentence.

B. **Life goals** – applying life vision to each specific area of life.

C. **Long-term goals** (over 20-30+ years) and **short-term goals** (3 months–3 years)

1. **Spiritually** (prayer time, fasting days, Bible study, etc.)

2. **Relationally** (family, friends, etc.)

3. **Vocationally.**

4. **Ministry**

5. **Economically**

6. **Physically**

7. **Rest**

D. **Action plan** – for each long and short-term goal in each area of your life.

E. **Schedule** – for each action plan. This is where our life vision is most easily derailed and lost.

Therefore it says, "Awake, O sleeper and arise from the dead, and Christ will shine on you." Look carefully then how you walk, not as unwise but as wise, making the best use of the time, because the days are evil. Therefore do not be foolish, but understand what the will of the Lord is. (Ephesians 5:14-17)

VI.   THE WOMB OF PROPHETIC VISION

A. Vision for a life in the Spirit is the most important aspect of the focused life.

B. This vision ***must*** be accompanied by an action plan. Many have the basic vision. Very few really enter into this reality.

C. The word and prayer are like a spiritual womb. They launch us into our destiny and the fullness of God.

VII.   DEVELOPING AN ACTION PLAN FOR THE WORD

A. How to develop an action plan in the Word. (3 options)

1. 10 chapters per day in the New Testament, 6 days per week. You will read the entire New Testament in 1 month. Repeat this and select verses to pray.

2. Make of list of most desired books of the Bible to study/pray/read. Use commentaries and journal. Then pray selected passages.

3. Read in multiple places.

B.   How to use commentaries

1.   Read 1-3 commentaries on the text. Underline or highlight key portions of the commentary.

2.   Journal on the insights from the commentary in your own words.

3.   Turn any revelation into prayer

4.   Internet resources – www.soniclight.com (click on study aids), www.ccel.org (old commentaries), www.otgateway.com,www.tyndale.cam.ac.uk/tyndale/links_biblical.htm#

anchortools, www.crosswalk.com, www.christiansunite.com (click on

bible study aids).

Now there was one, Anna, a prophetess, the daughter of Phanuel, of the tribe of Asher. She was of a great age, and had lived with a husband seven years from her virginity; and this woman was a widow of about eighty-four years, who did not depart from the temple, but served God with fastings and prayers night and day. And coming in that instant she gave thanks to the Lord, and spoke of Him to all those who looked for redemption in Jerusalem. (Luke 2:36-38)

So the child [John the Baptist] grew and became strong in spirit, and was in the deserts till the day of his manifestation to Israel. (Luke 1:80)

I.   TWO STRUCTURES

A.   In order to understand the prayer movement, both historic and present day, it is critical that one understand the ecclesiology (study of the church) of the monastic/missions movements.

B.   There are ***two structures*** that are necessary to complete the Great Commission. These two structures have always been present throughout church history, though they have taken many distinct forms and expressions:

1.   *Apostolic structures ("sodalities")* – This structure is focused on a specific missional/apostolic task. Examples of the sodalities are Paul's missions team, Jesus' team of disciples, monasteries, missions bases, city-wide ministries, universities, the Levitical priesthood, etc. Houses of prayer missions bases (as they are expressed in our context) are examples of this structure. They must be focused on an apostolic (God-given) assignment of day and night prayer and missions. They are, therefore, not ideal contexts for nurturing large communities of people over the long term. This structure, because of its intense nature, needs to be driven by teams of, essentially, full-time, vocational missionaries.

2.   *Local church structures ("modalities")* – This structure is focused primarily on nurturing the body of Christ over the *long-term*. Though local congregations are very much still focused on the "assignment" of the great commission, their methodology is very different in that the overriding concern is for individuals to be pastored and nurtured over the long term. This is the "parish" or congregational structure.

C.   These two structures are inseparable from one another. There is a strong overlap between the two. For example, the sodality does nurture people, especially those who are related to their assignment specifically. And local congregations do move out in apostolic assignments. Sometimes, both structures work in one organization or ministry. But simply recognizing the differences helps make sense of the prayer movement. In order to accomplish certain apostolic assignments (e.g. day and night prayer) it is necessary to have an almost "unbalanced" focus on the assignment, but that is why we must have the whole picture of the Body of Christ to fulfill our mission.

II.   INTERCESSORY MISSIONS

A.   The apostolic structure of a day and night house of prayer requires full-time intercessors and musicians. Going day and night, "in the spirit of the Tabernacle of David," requires a full-time community as well as a larger community in the marketplace surrounding it. This reality is being raised up in the earth as one of God's central strategies at the end of the age to complete the Great Commission.

B.   The idea of full-time musicians and intercessors is actually quite practical when you understand what happens in the context of day and night worship. This idea is new to many.

C.   I personally believe that the fullness of the Spirit that many are seeking will not come to manifestation without singers, musicians, and intercessors being in there rightful place.

D.   These full-time "intercessory missionaries" will only be less than one percent of the Body of Christ, but they are essential in this hour. This calling is not more important than any other assignment, but it is critical and widely misunderstood.

E.   Our missionaries at the Fredericksburg Prayer Furnace have very focused accountability. This vocation is not one that promotes laziness. Many of the hardest workers that I know are intercessory missionaries.

F.   In our context, full-time missionaries each have a "sacred trust" where they commit about 25 hours per week to the prayer room, where they are leading worship, engaging in intense intercession, or waiting on the Lord in meditative prayer and rigorous study. They also commit 20 hours every week to practical service and outreach in our region and the nations. These hours do not include weekly church meetings or our corporate gatherings. All things considered, most missionaries give about 50-60 hours per week to ministry.

G.   This is a unique calling. Many in the body of Christ have felt as if they are a "square peg in a round hole" in terms of their ministry calling. This is because the role of intercessory missions is not widely understood in protestant circles.

H.   God is also raising up a new breed of marketplace Christians, some of whom will embrace "prayer room" hours with a missions base as they are able.

III.   BIBLICAL AND HISTORICAL EXAMPLES

A.   Some would ask where this role is found in the Scriptures. This is a very legitimate question.

B.   One of the first examples is Anna. She was a prophetess and full-time intercessor in the temple ("day and night"). She was also the first evangelist in Jerusalem in the New Testament! Anna was undoubtedly with a company of others like her in the temple. Their fasting and prayer was a significant part of preparing for the coming of Jesus.

Now there was one, Anna, a prophetess, the daughter of Phanuel, of the tribe of Asher. She was of a great age, and had lived with a husband seven years from her virginity; and this woman was a widow of about eighty-four years, who did not depart from the temple, but served God with fastings and prayers night and day. And coming in that instant she gave thanks to the Lord, and spoke of Him to all those who looked for redemption in Jerusalem. (Luke 2:36-38)

C.   John the Baptist was a full-time intercessor for years. He lived in the wilderness for the purpose of fasting and prayer. This was the preparation for his manifestation as a voice to prepare for Jesus' first coming.

So the child [John the Baptist] grew and became strong in spirit, and was in the deserts till the day of his manifestation to Israel. (Luke 1:80)

For John came neither eating nor drinking… (Matthew 11:18)

D.   In the same way, God is raising up full-time forerunners in the wilderness of fasting and prayer in this hour. Once again, this is intensely practical. This kind of ministry requires this kind of preparation.

E. Paul actually took some years and dedicated them to the wilderness of fasting, prayer, and study. Scriptures do not indicate whether he was giving himself to the place of prayer and study full-time during this time, but there is little doubt that going deep in the knowledge of the Christ was his first pursuit during this time. He speaks of being "entrusted with the gospel!"

But when it pleased God, who separated me from my mother's womb and called me through His grace, to reveal His Son in me, that I might preach Him among the Gentiles, I did not immediately confer with flesh and blood, nor did I go up to Jerusalem to those who were apostles before me; but I went to Arabia, and returned again to Damascus. Then after three years I went up to Jerusalem to see Peter... (Galatians 1:15-18)

But as we have been approved by God to be entrusted with the gospel... (1 Thessalonians 2:4)

F. David financed 4,000 musicians and 288 singers to minister to the Lord full-time in the tabernacle. This was under the old covenant, but David's logic was actually more new covenant! He was motivated by extravagant love for the God of Israel and an awareness of the need for his manifest presence in Jerusalem. It is important to note that this kind of extravagance was unprecedented in Israel's history. It was the overflow of David's heart and was based on his understanding of what worship and prayer produced in the Spirit. Under the new covenant, how much more extravagant should we be!

G. The Lord said that he will cover the earth with incense (prayer and worship) in the days leading up to the second coming of Jesus! Malachi, when he prophesied this, certainly was thinking of full-time priests who would ministry day and night. There is really nowhere in the Scriptures that says that God ever desired this kind of extravagant worship to stop on the earth under the new covenant.

For from the rising of the sun, even to its going down, My name shall be great among the Gentiles; in every place incense shall be offered to My name, and a pure offering; for My name shall be great among the nations," says the LORD of hosts. (Malachi 1:11)

H. The Apostolic ministry required the lifestyle of an intercessory missionary as well.

Then the twelve summoned the multitude of the disciples and said, "It is not desirable that we should leave the word of God and serve tables. Therefore, brethren, seek out from among you seven men of good reputation, full of the Holy Spirit and wisdom, whom we may appoint over this business; but we will give ourselves continually to prayer and to the ministry of the word." (Acts 6:2-4)

I.   Historically, monasticism has been a cradle of this ministry of day and night worship and always necessitated full-time communities. For more information on the monastic movement, see "Session 4" of these notes.

J.   Many in the past, such as Rees Howells and David Brainerd, were called as full-time missionaries with a primary emphasis on prayer, intercession, and study.

K.   In this time, God is again raising up a "new monastic" missions movement. He is raising missionaries that are given to intercession and worship.

IV.   CONVERGENCE OF THE PRAYER AND MISSIONS MOVEMENTS

A.   There are three basic components of the missions movement in the nations of the earth.

    1.   Preaching (including writing and creative expressions of the gospel)

    2.   Mercy Deeds

    3.   Intercession

B.   Intercession has been, historically, the most neglected of the three and it requires full-time staff as much as the first two in order to practically function as it is meant to!

C.   At this time, the leaders of many of the primary missions organizations, such as YWAM and Campus Crusade for Christ, are recognizing the need for day and night prayer in order to complete the Great Commission in the nations.

D.   These missions leaders have recently approached some to the leaders of the prayer movement and begun to pursue dynamic partnership. The prayer movement is the missions movement! The missions movement is the prayer movement! YWAM, in particular, plans to begin to plant houses of prayer all over the earth!

E.   We need a house of prayer that contends against the Islamic house of prayer in the nations!

ADDENDUM 1

SONS OF THUNDER PROPHECY [32]
BY JAMES RYLE

The following word was shown to me beginning in August 1990 as a result of three dreams I had. In August, the Lord spoke to me through a dream. Prior to that dream He gave me a scripture, Isaiah 21:6, which says, "This is what the sovereign Lord says, 'Go appoint a lookout and have him report what he sees." When the Lord gave me that verse, He said, "I'm doing this in your life. I'm appointing you as lookout. You will see things, and when you see these things, you report them." I am now reporting to you what I have seen.

The first thing I saw in the dream was a flatbed trailer with a curtain behind it and two guitars on guitar stands sitting on the trailer. It looked like a stage but it wasn't a stage in a theatre; it was a mobile stage that could be moved into the streets or parks. This trailer was at a carnival or at a fairground. The two guitars were sitting on their guitar stands with the microphones in place and the curtain was there. The color of these guitars was the most vivid, electric blue that I could imagine. They were acoustic guitars and that caught my eye; you would never see an acoustic guitar that was electric blue.

I then saw that the curtain was the same color, and it captured my attention. As I stood and looked at it, two men came walking out from behind the curtain with sheet music in their hands. They were very excited as they looked at this, and they pointed out the different notes and the different measures, cadences and all the different features of this music. It was obvious that they could not wait to play this music. I looked over their shoulders and I could tell by looking at the music that it was a new song. It was not new like someone had just written it, but it was new in quality. In the dreams, my thoughts were, "This is new like the Beatles' music was new." When the Beatles appeared in the sixties it was a new sound and it took the world by storm. Whenever one of their songs came on, you would automatically turn it up; it had a special quality that caught your ear - it turned your head. It was the most arresting sound that our generation had ever heard. I remember looking at that sheet music in this dream and thinking that this music was going to be just like that, with one very significant distinction - this was of Christ.

I stood on that platform thinking - "Wait 'til these people hear this song!" I couldn't wait to see this happen, but the dream ended. After I had written the dream down, the Lord spoke to me and said, "I'm about to release a new kind of song in the streets. It will bring a revelation of the truth and it will usher men into my presence." I filed that away until about a month later when I had another dream.

---

[32] ©1991 **MorningStar Publications Inc.**

In the second dream, I was taken to a large church, which had a stage. There were rooms on either side of the stage. The room on the right side was the equipment room - it had pianos, micro-phones, speakers, cables, cymbals, and drums; it looked like a garage packed with stuff. I looked around and saw a power amplifier over in the corner. The amp was unplugged, the cord had been wrapped around it, and it was dusty like it had been sitting in the corner for a while. I dusted it off. What I then saw took my breath away.

I gasped with a sense of discovery but also dread because of what I was holding in my hand. I held the power amp that the Beatles had used. I knew in that moment that this box was the source of their sound and their power. I realized that people would do anything to have this amp. There are bands who for years have been looking for that sound - and for that power. They had been doing everything within their scope of imagination to get that power. Here it was and I was holding it in my hand. I felt hunted; I felt vulnerable; I felt that I was threatened. I knew that I could be hurt by those who would do anything for the amp. As I stood there holding it, I asked aloud this question, "What is it doing here?"

Suddenly I was out of the equipment room and standing behind the pulpit at this church, still holding the amp. The church had grown to five times the size that it was at the beginning of the dream. There was a balcony and the place was packed with people. As I looked at all these people (they were oblivious to my presence), a woman stood up in the middle of the church, and a light shone on her. She began singing a song of the Lord. Her voice filled the auditorium, and all she sang was this: "In the name of Jesus Christ the Lord we say unto you, be saved." She sang it over and over. She would turn to her right and sing, then turn to her left and sing; then she would turn behind her and before her and sing the same thing. As I watched her sing, it was like a wind blowing on a wheat field. These people began to swoon in the presence of God and men and women were collapsing in their seats, converted to Christ, just by the power of that song.

That was how the dream ended.

When I awoke, the Lord said that there was going to be a new and distinctive anointing and sound restored to music that will turn the heads and capture the hearts of men for Jesus Christ... Simply singing the truth in the name of Jesus Christ, "We say unto you be saved," will release the power of His Spirit in such an awesome display that men and women will collapse in their seats and be converted to Christ. But the Lord said that a key to this will be this new anointing He is about to give to His music. The Lord said that in 1970 He lifted the anointing for that extraordinary music that could arrest the attention of men, and for twenty years He has held it in His hand. He is about to release it again. He said that it does not belong to the world, it belongs to the church. That's why it (the amp) was in the church's equipment room, because it is part of the church's equipment.

Music does not belong to Satan, but he has stolen much of it and seeks to use it for his own evil purposes. Music was given to worship the Lord, but Satan has turned it for self-worship, which is the reason we tend to worship musicians, and they tend to require that people worship them. That is all part of the perversion of the fall. True worship and true music belong to Jesus Christ. They are given to His church to serve Him with. The anointing the Lord is about to release on music is going to sweep the world in a manner like the Beatles did when they first came out. It's going to be a music that is new in kind, new in sound, arresting in its content; it will stop traffic, and it will turn men's heads and capture their hearts, but this time it will do it for the Lord.

In this dream I saw the balcony scene when the Beatles first played on the Ed Sullivan Show. I saw the kids pulling their hair, crying... That is what I saw - the same emotion, the same devotion, the tears in the eyes and that earnest look of love and adoration on the faces, but this time they were crying for Jesus! When this anointing comes on the music He is about to give His church, and His servants step forth in true service and worship to Him with these gifts, He will display the Holy Spirit in such a way that it will bring that kind of adoration to the Son of God, not to the musicians or our own self-centeredness.

I know that there can be some misunderstanding with this Beatle connection, but that is how it was related to me in the dream and I later saw this principle related in the Scriptures. Psalm 68:18 reads: "You ascended on high, you led captivity captive and gave gifts to men - even among the rebellious..." "The earth is the Lord's and all it contains" (Psalm 24:1). It all belongs to Jesus Christ... The Lord makes His sun to shine on the just and the unjust. He makes His rain to come on the wicked and the righteous. Gifts and talents are given by the Lord, even though we may use them for evil. We are now on the threshold of a prophesied new move of God which will be precipitated by a musical revival that encircles the world. God is going to bring praise into the streets. The choir that preceded the army of Jehosaphat will once again lift up the banners and strike the chords, only this time they will turn the hearts of men to Jesus Christ and not to themselves. They won't be saying, "John, Paul, George, and Ringo," or, "I'm of Paul, I'm of Apollos, I'm an Evangelical, I'm a Baptist, I'm a Catholic, or I'm a Lutheran." This time the adoration will be to one person alone - Jesus.

I was then given a third dream. Again I was taken to this large church where I had seen the amplifier. This time the church was empty except for one man. He was up on the stage playing a keyboard and singing to the Lord. It was a beautiful song, and he was crying because of the tender exchange taking place between him and the Lord. He was writing the song right there, just making it up as he went. I was greatly moved by this song and the man's pure worship. I had a camera with me and I decided to take a picture of this to remember it.

I took two Polaroid pictures that came out immediately. When I looked at these pictures I was stunned because both of them were glowing with a golden light. I looked up and I then could see it on the man. The entire platform around him was also glowing like gold. I knew that it was the anointing of God. I went up to this man and said, "Brother look at this," but it startled him. He quickly turned the instrument off and stepped back. I said, "Look at this, look at the anointing of God that's on you." He looked at the pictures only for a second, and putting his hands in his pockets, he shrugged his shoulders and started kicking on the ground shyly saying, "Oh, gosh I didn't know you were here, I'm so embarrassed." As he was going on like this I just looked at him and asked, "What are you doing? You don't have to apologize for this - this is the anointing of the Lord." Immediately the dream changed.

I had these two photographs in my left hand and a parchment scroll in my right hand. I looked at that scroll and it was a letter written by an unknown soldier of the Salvation Army forty years ago. It was signed Unknown Soldier. I read this letter and it was a prophecy. It said that the time would come when the Lord God will release into the streets an army of worshipping warriors known as the "Sons of Thunder." They will bring forth praise into the streets that will birth evangelism and praise and give many children to God. I was duly impressed with this prophecy but I didn't know what to do with it or the photographs of the man worshipping. Suddenly, the dream changed one more time.

I was in the sky, about a hundred yards or so above the ground and I was over a highway. The highway was ten lanes wide and it only went in one direction. As far as I could see in both directions the highway was completely grid-locked, jam packed with Hell's Angels, shoulder to shoulder, wheel to wheel, just revving their motorcycles. I knew intuitively that this was the broad path that led to destruction; I knew that I was looking at lost humanity.

Then I saw on the side of the road, in single file, a group of motorcyclists who were the only ones moving. What caught my eye was that they were in single file and were moving in single file on the shoulder on this highway. They were headed towards a field that was about a mile and a half away. In the middle of this field there was a stone that was almost like the Washington Monument, but it wasn't that tall. It was a monolith-like stone, and I knew that these motorcyclists were headed toward it. I also knew that they were headed there for the purpose of touching it, because when they touched it they would receive power to come back and lead all of these Hell's Angels to Christ.

I felt that I also had to get to that stone, and that I had to be there when they got there. In the dream I was able to fly like an eagle, so I swooped down to get a closer look at the motorcyclists who were in the single file. I could see on the back of their jackets the words "Sons of Thunder." I knew that this was the army of worshipping warriors about which the unknown soldier from the Salvation Army had prophesied. I hastened over to this stone, but when I got there it was completely surrounded by officers of the law. They were locked elbow to elbow in riot gear with clubs and masks waiting for a big riot. My first thought was, "Oh NO! These guys are not going to let us get near the stone." I was so grieved. Then I had the thought that all that was necessary was for this parchment and these photographs to touch that stone; if they touched that stone the anointing that this prophecy spoke of and the anointing that I saw on that man of music would be released on these Sons of Thunder. They would then be empowered to go into the streets and turn the Hell's Angels to Christ.

So I started to walk past the line, but they wouldn't let me through either! Suddenly I got an idea - I took the parchment and I folded it into a paper airplane, put the photographs down in the crease in order to sail it over the heads of the officers in- to the stone. I knew that I would only have one chance and that I could not miss. The stone was so large that the only way I could miss would be to fall short. (This may be the most important issue for us. The only thing that can stop us is our stopping. Will we fall short or will we touch it?) I took the airplane with the photos and prophecy and let it fly. It flew as straight as an arrow. Just when it was about one foot from touching the stone the dream ended!

I desperately wanted to go back to sleep and finish the dream but I could not. Then the Lord began to speak to me about it. The Lord said that the stone which I saw was symbolic of Him ("The stone which the builders rejected..."), but that it was also symbolic of the monument that men have built to Him. These men now feel that they must protect that monument from the very people He is calling to Himself. The "officers of the law" stand in riot gear ready to defend the Lord from those that they don't think are worthy enough to come near Him. The Lord then said, "Say this to the man of music. Stop submitting to false humility. Stop apologizing for the anointing of God which is on you." There are many who in the privacy of their intimate times with the Lord sing the song of the Lord which is glorious. But when they come into the church or into the presence of people they let the fear of man choke the song. The Lord says "Stop it! You do not need to apologize for that anointing." It is the glory of God that rests on you and the Lord is saying that it is now time for you to bring forth that which He has put in your heart to do. Sing the song of the Lord for the salvation of the lost. And your ministry in this will begin at the burial site of the fear of men.

The Lord said, "Say this to the church: 'Stand in the light, lift up your voice and sing in the streets. Sing the simple message of the gospel - in the name of Jesus Christ the Lord, be saved. Lift up your voice as a witness to Christ and the Spirit of God will cause people to be converted'." The Lord said to the Sons of Thunder: "I'm not endorsing a motorcycle gang. That is not My point. These are symbols which speak of the issues involved. A motorcycle is a quick, agile means of transportation and represents those who rid themselves of their excess baggage. It can go where other vehicles cannot go."

The Lord is calling men and women into a ministry of evangelism that will take them places where the churches cannot go. And like the stigma associated with motorcycle gangs, there will be rejection and misunderstanding associated with this ministry. Some will not understand why they go into bars and associate with people who look demonic (and sometimes are), just as the Lord Himself was misunderstood for His associations. Even so, the word of the Lord to the Sons of Thunder was be in the world but not of it!

Then the Lord said, "Say this to the officers of the law: 'Put down your clubs and stop defending Jesus from people who you don't think are worthy enough to touch Him. Open your doors and let those people come in. Stop being so enamored by the monument that you take your eyes off the living stones."

Then the Lord said this, "The last call is a call to intercession." He said to me that the dream ended the way it did for an important reason. He wanted us to know that while it is going to happen, it is not happening yet. It's about to happen, and between now and when it does there is a call for intercession. When the prophecy of that unknown soldier of the Salvation Army of a generation ago and the vision of the anointed man of music are joined hand in hand by those who will intercede, and those two things touch the heart of Jesus through intercessory prayer, the anointing will be released on the Sons of Thunder. And the Sons of Thunder will be released into the streets. We will then see a worldwide move of the Spirit of God.

There are three groups that actually make up these Sons of Thunder. They are the musicians, the evangelists who are not musicians, and the musicians who are evangelists. Some who are musicians are being called to be a Son of Thunder even though they are not evangelists. Some are evangelists who are being called though they are not musicians. Of course, there are some who are both evangelists and musicians. In some cases there will be musicians on a flatbed trailer, drawing the crowds for the evangelists.

When the musicians who have dedicated themselves to the Lord Jesus Christ begin to play this new song, the Spirit of God is going to move in that crowd. The evangelists will touch these people and explain what is happening to them. The Sons of Thunder are both the musicians and the evangelists who work together.

ADDENDUM 2

SEVEN THEOLOGICAL PREMISES OF THE FORERUNNER MINISTRY
BY MIKE BICKLE

A.   Premise #1: There will be *"unique dynamics"* in the generation the Lord returns.

    1.   It will witness the *greatest demonstration of power* both God's and Satan's (Rev. 13). The three "supernatural generations" in Scripture are the generation of Moses (Ex. 7-10), the generation of the apostles, and the generation Jesus returns in which the miracles done by Moses and the apostles will be combined and multiplied on a global level.

    2.   It is the generation *most described* by God in His Word.

    3.   It is the generation that is *most populated*. Some estimate that there will be more people alive in this one generation in one life span (70 years) than in all history combined. After the Great Harvest, there will be more of God's people on earth than in heaven.

    4.   The greatest number of people at the time of the greatest manifestation of power will require a unique preparation, focus and understanding. The unique dynamics of the generation in which history transitions to the Millennial Kingdom is the "new thing".

    Do not remember the former things, nor consider the things of old. Behold, I will do a <u>new thing</u>, now it shall spring forth; shall you not know it? (Isaiah 43:18-19)

B.   Premise #2: The Spirit is emphasizing the *revelation of the Father* in bringing God's family to maturity. God will raise up those who release the Father's heart in the home, church, marketplace and government (Ps 68:5-6). The Spirit is also highlighting care for the fatherless (orphans, etc.).

    I will send you Elijah the prophet <u>before</u> the coming of the great and dreadful day of the LORD. And he will <u>turn the hearts of the fathers to the children, and the hearts of the children to their fathers</u>, lest I come and strike the earth with a curse. (Malachi 4:5-6)

C.   Premise #3: The Holy Spirit will emphasize *3 facets of the beauty of Jesus* as clearly seen in Scriptures that describe God's End-Time plans (Rev. 19; Mt. 24-25; Isa. 60-62). There will be no contradiction in Jesus' heart and ministry as He manifests His glory as a Bridegroom, King, and Judge. He does not suspend one attribute to exercise another.

1.   Jesus as a *passionate Bridegroom*: has great tenderness and deep desire for His people

2.   Jesus as a *powerful King*: releases power in confronting darkness and winning the lost

3.   Jesus as a *righteous Judge*: upholds the standards of conduct (holiness)

D.   Premise #4: Forerunners will participate in the *3 unprecedented activities of the Holy Spirit:*

1.   *To restore the First Commandment to first place* worldwide as the Church is prepared as a worthy Bride (Mt. 22:37; Rev. 19:7).

2.   *To gather the Harvest* through an unprecedented release of God's power (Rev. 7:9, 14).

3.   *To release Jesus' End-Time judgments* described in Revelation (Rev. 6; 8-9; 16).

    a.   *To remove everything that hinders love* in preparing the Church as a Bride. The principle of God's love in judgment: God uses the least severe means to reach the greatest number of people at the deepest level of love without violating our free will.

    b.   *To aid in gathering the Harvest* by bringing eternity to bear on the hearts of multitudes of lost humanity and by manifesting God's power.

    c.   *To release God's vengeance* on those who hate Jesus and persecute His people.

E.   God's End-Times judgment will shake 7 spheres of human life. *1) The heavens:* the sky, atmosphere, weather patterns; *2) The earth:* earthquakes, volcanoes, etc.; *3) The sea:* tidal waves, tsunamis, etc.; *4. The dry land:* vegetation and plant life; *5) All nations:* national and social infrastructures will be shaken; *6) Religious institutions:* multitudes come to Jesus as the Desire of All Nations; *7. Economic disruption:* commercial turmoil as God transfers wealth.

I will shake <u>heaven</u> and <u>earth</u>, the <u>sea</u> and <u>dry land</u>; and I will shake <u>all nations</u>, and <u>they shall come</u> to the Desire of All Nations, and I will fill this temple with glory…The <u>silver</u> is Mine, and the <u>gold</u> is Mine,' says the Lord of hosts. (Haggai 2:6-8)

F.   Premise #5: God is ***preparing forerunner ministries ahead of time*** in the wilderness that they may prepare others for the Day of the Lord activities. It takes a clear sense of mandate and identity as a forerunner to stay faithful long-term to grow in understanding (Dan. 11:33-35). God is raising up "friends of the Bridegroom" type forerunner ministries like John the Baptist who will fast and pray as they "stand and hear" Jesus' voice as the Bridegroom God.

   The friend of the Bridegroom, who stands and hears him, rejoices greatly because of the Bridegroom's voice. Therefore this joy of mine *(John the Baptist)* ***is fulfilled. (John 3:29)***

G.   Premise #6: Forerunners must ***live a fasted lifestyle*** in the grace of God as seen in Mt. 6:1-18. This is God's way to position ourselves to tenderize our hearts to receive <u>more</u> revelation in <u>faster</u> time frames with a <u>deeper</u> impact on our hearts.

H.   ***"For John*** *(the Baptist)* ***came neither eating nor drinking…" (Matthew 11:18)***

I.   Premise #7: Forerunners are ***best trained in context of a massive end-time prayer and worship movement***. God is raising up forerunner ministries in local congregations that are rooted in prayer that flows in the spirit of the Tabernacle of David.

   After this I will return and rebuild David's fallen tent. Its ruins I will rebuild, and I will restore it (Acts 15:16)

   Blow the trumpet in Zion, declare a holy fast, call a sacred assembly. (Joel 2:15)

ADDENDUM 3

Atomic Power with God (1946)

By REV. FRANKLIN HALL

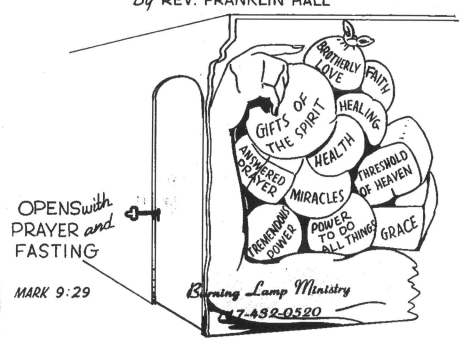

OPENS *with*
PRAYER *and*
FASTING

MARK 9:29

COPYRIGHT, REG. 1946
(NEW EDITION, COPYRIGHT, 1973)

19256255R00087

Made in the USA
Charleston, SC
14 May 2013